Stepping Stones

Stepping Stones
to a Global Ethic

Marcus Braybrooke

SCM PRESS LTD

ISBN 0 334 01574 X

First published 1992
by SCM Press Ltd,
26-30 Tottenham Road, London N1 4BZ

Typeset at The Spartan Press Ltd,
Lymington, Hants
and printed in Great Britain by
Mackays of Chatham, Kent

Contents

Preface   vii

PART I

1 The Search for a Global Ethic   3
2 The Interfaith Movement: The Present Reality   6
3 Are Human Rights based on Religious Traditions?   10
4 Religious Support for Human Rights   17
5 What do the Statements say?   21
6 Is Anyone Listening?   23

PART II

1 The Universal Declaration of Human Rights   27
2 Declaration on the Elimination of All Forms of Intolerance
   and of Discrimination Based on Religion or Belief   34
3 Fundamental Postulates of Christianity and Judaism in
   Relation to Human Order   38
4 Declarations of the World Conference on Religion and
   Peace   41
   I Kyoto, Japan 1970   42
   II Louvain, Belgium 1974   54
   III Princeton, USA 1979   68
   IV Nairobi, Kenya 1984   82
   V Melbourne, Australia 1989   94
5 Declarations of the International Association for Religious
   Freedom   107
6 Declaration on the Oneness of the Human Family   114

7	The Mt Abu Declaration	116
8	Declaration of Human Responsibilities for Peace and Sustainable Development	120
9	International Conferences on Peace and Non-Violent Action	124
	1 Ladnun Declaration	124
	2 Rajsamand Declaration	129
10	Global Survival	133
	1 Oxford Declaration	133
	2 Moscow Declaration	135
11	An Earth Charter	138
12	The World's Religions for the World's Children	143
13	The Universal Declaration on Non-Violence	147
	Notes	149

Preface

I am very grateful to the Gordon Cook Foundation and especially to its Chief Executive, Mr William Robb, for their support and interest. The Gordon Cook Foundation is an Aberdeen-based Educational Charity founded in 1974 to promote Values Education and Citizenship throughout the United Kingdom.

Once again, I express gratitude to Dr John Bowden and all the staff of SCM Press. My special thanks go to Sally Richmond for typing so meticulously all the documents and to my wife Mary for her encouragement. I am grateful to the various interfaith organizations who have produced these documents and have allowed me to reproduce them.

January 1992   Marcus Braybrooke

For
our granddaughter

Kathryn Elizabeth Hobin

In the hope that her generation
will discover how to live as a human family

PART I

I

The Search for a Global Ethic

'A Global Village' has become a common way to describe our world society, where instant communication and modern means of travel have created a world community. A characteristic of many villages is that the inhabitants share a similar world view, a culture, an ethic and perhaps a religion. In many villages, of course, there are often minorities, and today large numbers do not share in the opportunities of the Global Village. The Global Village excludes millions of poorer people in the way that Greek civilization excluded the slaves on whom the economy depended. Yet even those who are illiterate are affected by the decisions of world trade. A distant stock-market can decimate the value of a cash crop even more decisively than a plague of locusts.

Despite reservations about some of the implications of the term, the question which now faces the inhabitants of the Global Village is whether a world society needs a world view, a culture, an ethic and a religion. Prince Philip, in his Preface to Hans Küng's *Global Responsibility*, says that it has proved possible to arrive at a broad consensus about the facts of life on earth. Scientific discourse, like trade, is international. It has, however, Prince Philip continues, 'so far at least proved impossible to overcome the jealousies, rivalries and the destructive consequences of competing religions and ideologies'.[1]

Is it possible that a world ethic will emerge? Hans Küng himself says that 'the one world in which we live has a chance of survival only if there is no longer any room in it for spheres of differing, contradictory and even antagonistic ethics'. He concludes his book with this summary:

'No human life without a world ethic for the nations;
No peace among the nations without peace among the religions;
No peace among the religions without dialogue among the religions.'[2]

For nearly a century those in the interfaith movement have sought to encourage such dialogue among the religions. From small beginnings, interreligious dialogue now engages a growing number of people in all religions. A sketch of the development of the world-wide interfaith movement is given below. Part of the dialogue has been on ethical matters.

At a number of interfaith conferences, statements have been made affirming some shared values and sometimes making specific suggestions about moral behaviour. These statements are the subject of this book and summaries and extracts of the most important comprise the second part.

There are many questions. Do these statements draw deeply on the teachings and traditions of the world religions or have texts been found to give a cloak of religious respectability to ideas which derive from the enlightenment and the modern world? Human rights, for example, is in one sense a recent concept, but some would claim that it derives from the age-old moral teaching of the religions.

Does the apparent agreement in such statements mask the deep differences between religions? This book is not the place to speculate on the possibility of an emergent world religion to accompany a world society. Religions are complex entities and ethical behaviour is related to beliefs. These differ widely between religions. Is it possible to hope that the world religions may share values if they do not share beliefs?

How representative of their faith communities are those who produced or endorsed these statements? Even within religious traditions, there are sharp differences about belief, practice and behaviour. Is it not therefore a chimera to suggest that there can be agreement between religions? Do not the statements merely represent an agreement between 'liberals' of different religions? Often those who are deeply committed to interfaith exploration find themselves out of sympathy with their fellow believers.

In any case, if the religions do agree, what practical difference will this make? Religious influence has seldom made peace and has often aggravated conflict. Many people are disillusioned with religions and are not willing to base their behaviour on the teaching of a particular religious tradition. Yet, as Prince Philip says, 'The motivation for altruism seems to originate in a personal attachment to an ideology or to a religion. The evidence suggests that people are influenced in their behaviour by moral conviction and ethical concepts.'[3] Even so, many are reluctant to be told what to do by a religious authority. The ethical teaching of a faith community needs to commend itself as life-enhancing. In Hans Küng's words: 'The fundamental criteriological ethical question can be formulated: What is good for human beings . . . the basic ethical criterion is: Humans should not live inhumanly.' Religions should, he suggests, be able to agree that 'the good for human persons is what helps them to be truly human'.[4]

Supposing such agreement is possible between the religions, how then is the world ethic communicated to the citizens of the world? More particularly, how are people best educated in moral values, especially young people?

The search for a new world ethic raises many questions and implies a far-reaching programme. Whilst some of these questions will be discussed a little more fully below, they will not be answered. The documents may provide raw material for such answers or at least be a litmus test for theories. Some people belonging to different faith traditions have been able to agree on some ethical issues. Is their work a sign of hope for the future?

The Interfaith Movement: The Present Reality

The hope that religious people could together affirm certain moral principles was in the minds of some of those who attended the World's Parliament of Religions in Chicago in 1893. Charles Bonney, whose idea the Parliament was, said that one object was 'to make the Golden Rule the basis of the union (of religions) and to present to the world . . . the substantial unity of many religions in the good deeds of the religious life'.[1] At the Parliament the contribution of religion to peace and social issues was fully covered.

Regarded now as the beginning of the interfaith movement, the Chicago World's Parliament has come to symbolize the aspirations of all who believe that religious people should be friendly and cooperative to one another and work together for human welfare and peace. The Parliament's immediate impact, however, was more ephemeral. The Parliament drew American public attention to the teachings and practices of religions other than Christianity. It also gave an impetus to the emerging study of world religions.

The momentum for interreligious understanding and cooperation has steadily gathered pace since the 1893 Parliament, although no continuing organization emerged from the World's Parliament of Religions. At first slowly and recently quite rapidly, interfaith groups have been established in many places. Some are quite small, meeting in a home. Other interfaith organizations are national bodies and some are international, seeking to coordinate global interfaith concern.

Some of those who attended the World's Parliament of Religions helped to found **The International Association for Religious Freedom** (IARF). There are many differences among members of the International Association for Religious Freedom, but all are united by a commitment to religious freedom and truthful living. The IARF supports social service projects through its member groups. It is increasingly championing human rights and has representatives at the United Nations. IARF Congresses are held every three years. Some of the documents in Part II derive from such congresses.

The World Congress of Faiths (WCF) was founded in 1936 by Sir Francis Younghusband. In 1903, in Lhasa, Tibet, he had a decisive spiritual experience of an underlying unity of all beings. His hope was that through WCF members of all religions would become aware of the universal experience which had been his and that 'the roots of fellowship would strike down deep to the Central Source of all spiritual loveliness'.[2] During the Second World War, he pleaded for people of all religions to share in creating a world loyalty. One of his successors as chairman, Lord Sorensen, whilst admitting that moral patterns vary considerably, insisted that there were moral values affirmed by all faiths.[3]

The Temple of Understanding (ToU), now based in New York, was founded in 1960 by Judith Hollister. The hope, as yet unfulfilled, has been to build a temple that would symbolize the shared spiritual quest of all religions. Meanwhile the organization has done much to foster the spirit of understanding. The Temple has held a series of Summit Conferences to parallel political summits, because in Judith Hollister's words, 'people spend hours at the conference table – but no time in trying to understand what is going on in the other man's mind'.[4] The Temple has had an international influence through contacts with delegates to the United Nations. It also helped to give birth to the Global Forum on Human Survival. The Temple has produced a document on 'The Oneness of the Human Family', which is printed in Part II.

Whilst the efforts of these organizations have helped to promote a climate of peace, some interfaith organizations, especially **The World Conference on Religion and Peace**, have concentrated on encouraging religious people to be active in peace work. WCRP has seen that it is important that leaders of the world's religions should affirm together their concern for peace and human dignity. Religious people should be more aware of the major issues facing humankind, especially as they are reflected in the concerns of the United Nations.

Five assemblies have been held. Each assembly has issued a declaration and these appear in Part II. There have also been commissions and working parties; many of their reports are of interest and are summarized below.

It is hard to assess the impact that religious people can have on political processes, especially as politicians seldom acknowledge those who have influenced them. Modern communications have given added weight to popular opinion. Religious leaders may play an important role in forming public opinion. They can insist on the relevance of spiritual and moral considerations. They have helped to maintain public alarm at the enormous stockpile of nuclear weapons and other means of mass destruction. They have voiced public outrage at the starvation of millions of people, as a result of hunger, war, injustice and an unfair pattern of international trade. They have upheld human dignity and protested against torture and racism. They have underpinned efforts to develop internationally agreed standards of human rights and have helped to monitor their application. Interreligious conferences have been among the first to warn of threats to the environment.

In local areas of conflict, religious people have often maintained contact across boundaries and divisions. Sometimes they have been agents of reconciliation and conflict-resolution. They have taken a lead in relief work. Sometimes they have encouraged acts of repentance in an effort to heal deeply rooted bitterness. Yet often, too, religious people have used religious loyalties to inflame conflict and have allowed particular interests to outweigh common human and religious moral values. Some extremists stir up religious passions to gain support for their concerns.

Slowly the value of interfaith dialogue has become more widely recognized. In 1966, the Second Vatican Council's decree *Nostra Aetate* transformed the Catholic Church's attitude to people of other religions. A Secretariat for Non-Christians was established, which is now called The Pontifical Council for Inter-Religious Dialogue. At much the same time, the World Council of Churches established a Unit for Dialogue with People of Living Faiths, which has arranged various consultations. Many religious and denominational bodies now have agencies to encourage such dialogue. There are some official discussions between religions. Clearly, official dialogue has a character of its own. Participants have some representative role. Much of the work is to remove misunderstanding and build up good relations, but emphasis has also fallen on encouraging practical cooperation on moral issues and social concerns. Indeed the search for shared moral values may be more appropriate to official discussions than more speculative dialogue about questions of 'truth'.

The Gulf War and the Salman Rushdie affair have emphasized the practical importance and urgency of interfaith understanding. No longer can anyone dismiss religion as obsolescent or irrelevant to world affairs. But many wonder whether the future belongs to the interfaith movement or whether we are likely to see increasing religious rivalry. Some indeed picture the next century being dominated by renewed conflict between Christendom and the world of Islam. It is only three hundred years ago that the Turks were at the gates of Vienna.

To meet the contemporary challenge, the interfaith movement needs to become more practical. Religious rivalries destroy lives. If the interfaith movement is successfully to oppose the forces of religious extremism, there needs first to be repentance of the rivalry and hostility which have soured religious relations through the centuries.

Secondly, religious people should fearlessly unmask the misuses of religion. Too often religion has been used to cloak abuses of power. Religious people need to make clear that their commitment to the search for truth and the defence of human rights is stronger than their group loyalty – costly as this may be.

Thirdly, the emphasis has to be on the search for a global ethic. The discovery of those who attended the first meeting of the World Conference on Religion and Peace in Kyoto, Japan, in 1970 was that 'the things which unite us are more important than the things which divide us'.[5] The interfaith organizations have shown that people of many religions, whilst disagreeing about beliefs, can agree on the importance of peace and justice, of social action to relieve suffering and on efforts to save the planet. In promoting 1993 as a 'Year of Interreligious Understanding and Co-operation', they hope to show the importance of interfaith work not only in combating extremism and communalism but in harnessing the energies of all people of faith and of good will to tackle the urgent problems of the world.

3

Are Human Rights based on Religious Traditions?

In one sense human rights seem to be a new concern. Only in recent years has the world community challenged the behaviour of governments in the name of human rights. Even now the world community is reluctant to interfere in the 'internal' affairs of a sovereign state – even when genocide is taking place. Yet it can be claimed that human rights are grounded in faith traditions. Indeed Louis Henkin suggests that today 'all the major religions proudly lay claim to fathering human rights'.[1] This is in contrast to the suggestion sometimes made that religions are merely trying to give religious sanction to ideas that derive from other sources – or, to put the criticism more crudely, that human rights concerns are just 'the religious flavour of the month'.

The development of human rights owes much to the struggle for constitutional rights in Europe and the USA. It is therefore based on Western civilization, which in turn rests on Graeco-Roman civilization which developed the idea of natural law, and on Judaeo-Christian religion which taught that every person was made in the image of God. The frameworks of other civilizations and religions were different, but there too there were ideas which could be developed to support human rights.

The Universal Declaration of Human Rights

There is a long prehistory to the Declaration of Human Rights.[2] This reaches back in Britain to Magna Carta (1215) and to the 1689 Bill of Rights that followed 'The Glorious Revolution', when King James II was deposed from the throne of Britain. In America, it is evident in the Bill of Rights of the Constitution of Virginia and in the American Declaration of Independence. In France, the Declaration of the Rights of Man was promulgated soon after the storming of the Bastille in 1789. The Second World War was the gestation period for the Universal Declaration of Human Rights. President Franklin D. Roosevelt in January 1941 spoke of four freedoms on which world society should be founded: freedom of speech and expression, freedom of religion, freedom from want, and freedom from fear. 'Roosevelt,' writes Theo C.van Boven, 'was explicit in stressing that these freedoms were to be secured everywhere in the world, that is to say, on a universal basis. He made it clear that traditional freedoms of speech and worship should go hand in hand with such wider human rights as economic and social welfare and peace and security for all peoples and persons.'[3] A year later, the Allied Powers – in what was sometimes called 'The Declaration of the United Nations', since the Allied Powers called themselves the United Nations – claimed that total victory was necessary 'to defend life, liberty, independence and religious freedom and to preserve human rights and justice in their own lands as well as in other lands'.[4] Religious leaders in the USA, with some support from Britain, backed this and themselves drew up 'The Three Faith Declaration' on post-war reconstruction.[5]

When the United Nations Charter was framed in San Francisco in 1945, Article 1 stated that among the purposes of the UN is 'to achieve international cooperation . . . in promoting and encouraging respect for human rights and for fundamental freedoms for all without distinction as to race, sex, language or religion'.[6] This was not, however, felt to be enough and it was agreed to spell out human rights in the 1948 Universal Declaration of Human Rights, which is reproduced in the second part of this book.

Origins in Western civilization

Greek thinkers such as Plato, Aristotle and the Stoics developed the idea of natural law, under the jurisdiction of which all humans fell. Every citizen in Greek society had rights simply as a matter of birth – but these did not extend to slaves, children or women. The Romans greatly extended the role of law, but, rather than applying Roman civil law to the peoples whom they conquered, they tried to preserve their subjects' indigenous laws. Even so, the Romans held that many fundamentals of law applied to all nations. The third century Roman Jurist Gaius called this *ius gentium*, or 'the common law of all humans'.[7]

The concept of human rights also grows out of the Judaeo-Christian religious tradition. The Bible affirms that all life derives from and is dependent on God, the Creator. God made men and women in his image, thereby giving them an inalienable dignity. 'Regardless of our exegesis of that richly ambiguous term,' writes the American Reform rabbi Eugene B. Borowitz, 'there is something about every human being which is identified with the absolute source of value in the universe'.[8] Further, through the covenant, God called the people of Israel into partnership with himself and commanded them to create a holy society.

The detailed regulations of a holy society are reflected in the first books of the Bible and they show concern for the disadvantaged – for the orphan and widow. Perhaps very particularly this sense of an inalienable human dignity is shown in the treatment of the stranger or 'sojourner'. The law insists that 'you must not oppress the stranger, for you know the heart of the strangers, having yourselves been strangers in the land of Egypt' (Exodus 23.9). Again, the law says: 'The stranger who resides with you shall be to you as one of the homeborn. You shall love him as yourself, for you were strangers in the land of Egypt. I am the Lord, your God' (Leviticus 19.33). God himself defends the powerless – an affront to them is an affront to God (cf. Matthew 25.31–46).

The prophets, therefore, believed themselves to speak in the name of God when they upheld the needs of the marginalized and reproved the rich and powerful and even kings. William A. Irwin says of the prophet Amos: 'His enlarged concept of the nature and authority of God evidently was rooted in a feeling of common human rights, pervasive beyond the political and religious boundaries of the time. This principle was for him embodied in the person of the God of Israel.'[9]

John the Baptist and Jesus stood in this tradition. Luke tells us that at the start of his ministry Jesus identified with the words of Isaiah: 'The Spirit of the Lord is upon me, because he hath anointed me to preach the gospel to the poor; he hath sent me to heal the brokenhearted, to preach deliverance to the captives, and recovering of sight to the blind, to set at liberty them that are bruised, to preach the acceptable year of the Lord' (Luke 4.19). Jesus in his ministry both taught about God's forgiving love for all and identified with the outcasts of society – thus again affirming that every person is precious in the eyes of God.

The concern for human dignity is evident both in the Jewish rabbinic tradition and in the teachings of the church. The Liberal Jewish scholar Claude Montefiore suggested some years ago that the 'prophets point forward on the one hand to the Law, which sought by definite enactment and discipline to help on the schooling of the holy nation, living apart and consecrated to God, and on the other to the apostle of Tarsus, who carried the universalistic idea to its final and practical conclusion'.[10] David Daube gives many examples of the roots of human rights in rabbinic literature.[11] The rabbis also taught that God had entered into a covenant with the whole human race through Noah. Certain laws were binding on all people: namely the prohibition of idolatry, blasphemy, murder, theft, sexual immorality and eating a limb severed from a living animal, as well as the positive injunction to establish courts of justice. Several major Jewish festivals, such as Passover which recalls the Exodus from Egypt, affirm the human right to political liberty.[12]

The New Testament, with its emphasis on Jesus' 'new command' to love one another, speaks more in terms of principle and motivation rather than by giving specific rulings. The Sermon on the Mount sets a high ideal, even if Christians have not lived up to it. Paul recognized that human rights did not imply unbounded individualism. J. Robert Nelson argues that Paul's teaching that the gifts of the Spirit should be used for the good of the community is 'an exemplary instance of the application of human rights within a communal context'.[13]

Islam

Islam does not regard itself as a new religion dating from the time of the Prophet Muhammad. Rather Islam – in the sense of obedience to God – began with the first man Adam. Muhammad is the last in the line of prophets dating back to Abraham and including Moses and Jesus. The Qur'an says: 'If you have any doubt over what we have revealed to you, seek among those of our messengers whom we sent before you' (43.45). The Qur'an, therefore, claims to repeat the ethical teaching of the Bible and should be read in that context.

Human rights in Islam are therefore based on the sovereignty of God. It is God who guarantees the sanctity and dignity of human life. Every being has an end willed by God. 'Our Lord has bestowed on each thing his form and his law (*gadar*), and he has guided it towards its full blossoming' (87.13).

Human beings alone are free to obey or disobey divine law. Prophets have been sent to every nation reminding people of God's will. There is no doctrine of original sin in Islam. It is assumed that people are able to understand the divine will and freely able to obey or disobey.

Much of the Prophet's concern was with shaping a community (*umma*) which was obedient to God. This community was not founded on blood or race, nor on commercial links nor even on a common language. The community is based solely on faith, on unconditional obedience to the will of God. The community is potentially universal and Islam has been able to bond together people of every race and colour. Nation states, although they exist in the Islamic world, are essentially alien to the idea of the *umma*.

The whole of life is governed by the *Sharia*, the divine law. 'It governs,' writes Roger Garaudy, 'by its principles all human relationships, from economics to politics and from the inner life to conjugal relations, from the perspective of faith in an omnipresent and omniscient God whom no one can deceive. The *Sharia* then consists of living one's public and private life, twenty-four hours a day, in the sight of Allah.'[4] The *Sharia* or law of Islam derives from the Qur'an, but more in terms of principles than detailed regulations. Although the law may be unchanged, circumstances and therefore its application change. Various schools came into existence, each with rather different interpretations, drawing in part upon the collections of the sayings and actions of the Prophet (*hadith*).

Whilst, like the Bible, the Qur'an does not specifically speak of 'human rights', it too sees human life as a gift of God, who sets standards for human behaviour.

Hinduism

Just as in Judaism, Christianity and Islam the meaning of life derives from God the giver of life, so traditionally Hindu society was shaped by the transcendent goal of life. Bithika Mukerji writes: 'In India, lawgivers are seen to address themselves to the task of organizing a society to uphold justice and establish peace and yet at the same time to be open to the quest for transcendence of the human condition itself. The Hindu tradition can only be understood as a way of life which tries constantly to keep the supreme human duty of self-enlightenment or, in the language of religion, God-realization, at the centre of attention. Further, it can be seen that it is here, in the region of the human quest for supreme felicity, that ethical concerns and religious commitments become united, because the fulfilment of the quest waits upon the grace of the Ultimate Being or Brahman.'[5]

This quest is not confined to this life, but, through a series of reincarnations, may span many lives. One's progress is determined by *karma*, by how one lives. 'A man becomes good by good deeds and bad by bad deeds' (Brhadaranyaka IV, iv, 5).

The transcendental goal of life is shown in the four traditional stages of life: the period of study and discipline (*brahmacarya*); the duties of a householder (*grhastha*); retirement, when husband and wife are free from major responsibilities and can retire into the forest (*vanaprastha*); and abandonment of the world to live as a holy ascetic (*sannyasa*). These four stages were intended to lead a man progressively to perfection.

Traditionally society was organized on the caste system. Scripture speaks of four castes: of *Brahmana*, priests; *Ksatriya*, knights; *Vaisya*, traders; and *Sudra*, those who work on the land. 'The underlying principle,' wrote T.M.P. Mahadevan, 'is division of labour.'[6] It was based on mutal obligation. In practice caste divisions are numerous and the reality bears little resemblance to the scriptural ideal. Each caste had particular duties and an expected pattern of life.

Dharma, which includes moral behaviour as well as ritual practices, was the means to the highest goal of *moksa*, spiritual freedom or God-realization. 'Morality,' Mahadevan wrote, 'is desirable because it is the gateway to religion.'[17] Behaviour to others, whilst it may have a divine sanction, is therefore governed by concern for one's own spiritual progress, not because of inherent rights of the other.

Buddhism

Buddhism does not talk about one absolute God nor about specifically 'human' rights. Rather, Buddhism teaches the law of dependent co-origination, which emphasizes that everything in the universe is inter-dependent, co-arising and co-ceasing. There are no individual selves or entities (*Anatman*). The teaching of suchness or as-it-is-ness (*Tathata*) implies 'complete distinction and complete equality', writes Professor Masao Abe.[18] The Buddha taught the Middle Way, which rejected the extremes of sensual indulgence and of asceticism.

Strictly speaking, Masao Abe continues, 'rights' in Buddhism are not confined to humans, but include all living beings. Whilst at a relative level we have a sense of individuality, at the absolute level our individuality interfuses with other selves, with nature and with the divine. The command 'not to destroy life' includes not only 'human rights' but the rights of animals and plants. Compassion and wisdom extend to all beings. This emphasis on non-violence (*ahimsa*) towards all living beings is also to be found in Jainism.

This is personified in the Bodhisattva. This ideal 'in its concern for fellow beings, demonstrates the best concrete illustration of the doctrine of relational origination – in which every being is involved in every other being . . . It is not only the beginning of harmony with other beings, but more important, the sustenance of harmony within the changing ambient world.'[19]

Confucius

Confucius' emphasis was on the Way of Heaven (*Tao*) in which all people should walk. Ethics are central to his teaching, and he was mainly responsible for the moral principles at the basis of family, social and political life in China.

Conclusion

The development of human rights can be seen to relate to the Judaeo-Christian tradition, although the emphasis was more on duties and obligations to others. Human dignity was dependent on belief in the Creator. The same is true of Islam. In Hinduism, responsibilities to others related to the search for God-realization. In Buddhism, by contrast, human interdependence followed from the Buddhist analysis of reality.

Whilst scriptural texts can be found to support particular human rights, the search for religious sanctions for human rights needs deeper study. What is required is a search for the underlying understanding of human nature in each religious tradition and the attempt to see how such an understanding relates to the contemporary world. Already work is being undertaken to achieve this.

4

Religious Support for Human Rights

Increasingly a concern for human rights is becoming evident within each major religious tradition, as Dr R. Traer has shown in his valuable book *Faith in Human Rights*.[1]

Yet, even if it can be argued that religions do provide a sanction for human rights, many violations of human rights have been perpetrated in the name of religion. Religious bodies too have often been slow to espouse human rights issues. It is important to distinguish religious teaching and ideals from the behaviour of practitioners.

Abba Hillel Silver admits that: 'Religion was not only tardy in championing human rights; at times it was actually retarding and reactionary.'[2] Eric Weingartner also says that the 'Christian church has not historically been in alliance with the pioneers of human rights, whatever their tradition'.[3] Pope Pius VI in 1791 criticized the French Revolution's Declaration of the Rights of Man for supporting freedom of opinion and communication. In India traditional religion has often sanctioned cruel oppression in the name of the caste system. In many societies, religious authorities have countenanced the subordination of women.

In recent years, however, the World Council of Churches, which brings together Protestant, Anglican and Orthodox churches, has strongly advocated human rights, even if this at times has alienated some members of its participating churches. From the time of Pope Leo XIII (1878–1903), the Roman Catholic Church has increasingly engaged with developments in social and political life, although there are continuing tensions between the Vatican and the liberation theologians of Latin America. At the time of the depression and the rise of Fascism and Communism, Pope Pius XI (1922–1939) developed the notion of social justice and Pope Pius XII (1939–1958), at the height of the war, affirmed that human dignity required 'respect for and the practical realization of . . . fundamental personal rights'.[4] John XXIII (1958–1963) spoke in *Mater et Magistra* (1961) of human dignity in social and structural terms, and in *Pacem in Terris* (1961) affirmed the protection of human rights as the basis for world peace. 'Any human society,' he said, 'if it is to be well ordered and productive, must lay down as a foundation this principle, namely, that every human being is a person, that is, his nature is endowed with intelligence and free will. Indeed, precisely because he is a person he has rights and obligations flowing directly and simultaneously from his very nature. And as these rights are universal and inviolable so they cannot in any way be surrendered.'[5] Vatican II in *Dignitatis Humanae Personae* and in *Gaudium et Spes* affirmed these developments.

A concern for human rights is to be found also amongst conservative Christians, and is shown in practical action and struggle by Christians of many traditions and in many parts of the world. 'One might conclude,' writes Robert Traer, 'that the leadership of the human rights movement in Latin America, and around the globe, is in its churches, rather than in its law schools or political parties. For the churches worldwide have made human rights a central part of their Christian witness in societies where brutal violations of human rights and the basic conditions of human dignity are tragically commonplace.'[6]

The concern is not confined to the churches

After the Second World War, Jews joined with Christians in lobbying for the United Nations Charter and for the Universal Declaration of Human Rights. Because Jews have so often been denied basic human rights, even in this century the right to live, they have played an active part in contemporary human rights struggles.

Muslim countries too throughout the world have ratified international human rights covenants, although the government of Saudi Arabia initially abstained when the UN approved the Universal Declaration of Human Rights. The Emir of Kuwait, for example, has affirmed that 'to preserve the dignity of man, it is necessary that society guarantees him food, drink, lodging, clothing, education, and employment as well as his right to express his opinion, participate in the political life of his country and to be assured of his own security and that of his kin.'[7]

Many Hindu reformers, inspired by their religion, have challenged traditional practices. Rammohan Roy, founder of the Brahmo Samaj, advocated equality for all persons regardless of caste or sex, on the grounds that all humans are God's creatures. Vivekanda, the founder of the Ramakrishna Movement, dedicated himself to the service of 'My God the wicked, My God, the afflicted, My God the poor of all races'.[8] Mahatma Gandhi was fearless in seeking the rights of the untouchables, whom he called *Harijans* or children of God. Also in India, the Sikh Gurus challenged the caste system, and in this century Ambedkar turned to

Buddhism in his struggle for the depressed classes. More recently, partly because of the horrors of the Vietnam War, some Buddhists have become more socially active and a Network of Engaged Buddhists has recently been formed. Jainism, which had an influence on Gandhi, has long taught *ahimsa* or non-violence to all life.

Through the centuries there have been individuals inspired by their faith to struggle for peace, justice and human welfare, but all too often religious leaders were closely linked to the political authorities and used divine sanctions to support repressive regimes. Today, however, in every religion, there are those who are inspired by their faith to advocate and work for human rights. Increasingly they have the support of religious leaders. Many of those who are active in the struggle for human rights are also active in interfaith cooperation. Indeed it seems that those who seek cooperation with members of other faiths often find themselves critical of the conservatism and social indifference of many of their co-believers. Perhaps being open to interfaith contacts also makes people more aware of the failings of their religious community.

Is there any consensus?

Yet even if there is a growing emphasis on human rights in many religious communities, is there any consensus? The world view of each religious tradition is different and ethical concerns are set in particular frameworks.

Dr Traer writes: 'Understandings of human rights developed in liberal, socialist and Third World contexts may be seen as different emphases within a common tradition of faith. The tradition is grounded in the Universal Declaration of Human Rights, which is accepted by all as the foundation for human rights law. Moreover this tradition continues to develop, especially due to concerns in the Third World . . . Clearly members of different religious traditions affirm human rights as a part of their faith. To be sure these affirmations differ; however, these differences occur not only between the traditions but also within a particular tradition . . . However, it is clear that among those who affirm human rights there is considerable agreement as to both the fundamental importance of human rights in the modern world and the content of human rights. Furthermore, the Universal Declaration of Human Rights is affirmed within all the major world religious traditions, and religious leaders and institutions are working cooperatively around the globe for the protection of human rights through law. Thus faith in human rights is not merely international but interreligious.'9

John Milbank, on the other hand, argues that the good causes of socialism, feminism, anti-racism and ecologism have to be rooted in the

Western religious tradition. He argues that 'a postmodern position that respects otherness and locality, and yet at the same time still seeks the goals of justice, peace and reconciliation, can only, in fact, be a Christian (or possibly a Jewish) position'.[10] The question of theoretical support in all religions for human rights is therefore linked to questions about the relationship of religions. Is there any commonality between religions which transcends their obvious differences? There is an enormous and growing literature on this subject, but it may be, as Paul Knitter suggests, that it is by cooperation on human rights and liberation issues that the commonality will be discovered.[11] Certainly, the evidence of the World Conference on Religion and Peace and of some other interfaith gatherings is that agreement on practical concerns is possible, even if there is no theoretical basis for such agreement.

Hans Küng has suggested that a theoretical universal ethical criterion may be the basis for agreement. Whilst within each religious community there are accepted sources of authority, he points out that these are not accepted by people outside that community. If a moral injunction is to have universal appeal, it requires a universal criterion. Küng himself suggests that the *Humanum*, namely, whatever helps people to be truly human, is such a basic ecumenical criterion. He recognizes that there is no agreement about what constitutes the truly human, but the search for such agreement constitutes the agenda for the future.[12]

In attempting to make common affirmations and statements about human behaviour, some members from all religions have already, through interfaith conferences, started on this agenda. The second part of this book contains a selection of such statements. They are evidence that agreement is possible between some members of all faiths and provide a material basis for theoretical analysis. They are the first footpaths of interfaith pioneers. The religious communities now need to provide the resources to make of these paths highways to a future in which all people have the possibility of a truly human life.

5

What do the Statements say?

Some people of all religions affirm that as people of faith they have a responsibility and right to speak on major human issues. Religion should not be divorced from politics. It is not only an inward and individual concern but should seek to shape society in obedience to God's will. It is noteworthy that this is said by members of Indian religious traditions as well as by Jews, Christians and Muslims. The Ladnun Declaration of Anuvrat has a section on political action (see pp. 124ff.). In the Buddhist world, as already mentioned, a Network of Engaged Buddhists has been established.

It is frequently claimed, for example at the Oxford Conference of Christians and Jews (see pp. 38ff.), that morality has a religious basis, although Hans Küng admits that a moral life is possible without religion.[1] Some statements claim that there is a universal moral law. Others insist that religions uphold the sacredness of the individual.

It is recognized repeatedly that religion has frequently been misused and that still today it is often used to cloak oppression and discrimination. Violent conflict is in many places exacerbated by religious differences.

Even so, the documents insist that religion should be a power for peace. The possession of nuclear weapons is condemned in increasingly strong terms. There is little sympathy for arguments about the 'balance of terror'. The horrible suffering caused by all weapons is recognized. There are particular warnings about chemical weapons, calls for an end to the arms trade and for the abolition of war-toys. There is detailed discussion of the way of non-violence and an emphasis on the strength of love to change the world.

It may seem that this stress on peace and non-violence does not grapple fully with the power of evil and injustice. How is cruel oppression to be defeated? The documents recognize that injustice is a cause of violence. They speak strongly in defence of human rights and vigorously oppose racism and apartheid and other forms of discrimination, especially against women.

The answer to oppression would seem to lie in strengthening the

United Nations. Several documents suggest the UN should have the right to interfere in the 'internal affairs' of a country where there is a threat of genocide or serious injustice. This would imply a change to present international law. There is some suggestion that the concept of crimes against humanity should be developed so that there is an international tribunal at which tyrants could be arraigned. It is said that everyone should have the right to resist an unjust order and that the right to conscientious objection should be upheld in every country.

Poverty as well as social justice is recognized as a major threat to peace. 'Liberation plus development equals peace', said the Louvain Declaration (p. 56). The arms race is seen to waste enormous resources which should be used to meet human need. The greed and exploitation of rich nations is condemned, as well as unfair patterns of international trade. There is a general assumption that the wealth of the few is at the expense of the poverty of the many, which is a view that might be questioned by some economists. There is widespread suspicion of multinational companies. The need to control the growth of the world's population is generally recognized, although there is disagreement about whether artificial methods of birth control are morally acceptable.

Environmental concerns occupy increasing attention, and a body devoted to this, The Global Forum on Human Survival, has recently been established. Yet this is not a new concern. Anxiety about despoiling natural resources was voiced at the Oxford Conference of Christians and Jews in 1946 (p. 39), and in the Kyoto declaration of the First Assembly of WCRP (p. 47).

Awareness of the interrelatedness of all life has reinforced the stress on human interdependence and on calls for co-operation – in contrast to the competitive spirit encouraged by some politicians and by the capitalist system. The dissatisfaction of some religious people with many aspects of capitalism suggests that with the collapse of communism, more attention will need to be given to alternative economic systems which are not so exploitative of people and nature.

Interdependence and co-operation imply that we all have responsibilities towards each other to promote the common good. Recent documents, especially the Costa Rica declaration (pp. 121f.) have stressed that human rights have to be matched by human responsibilities. Maybe, in championing human rights, religious people have a special contribution to make in teaching human responsibilities. They are a significant aspect of the search for shared moral values.

6

Is Anyone Listening?

Many people, especially the young, are disillusioned with religion. They reject traditional authority and feel that religion calls for behaviour which is out of touch with modern life. To many, religion is a term which suggests extremism, fanaticism and obscurantism. Meanwhile the Communist alternative has collapsed, and a growing number are disenchanted with the competitive materialism of capitalist society. Yet at the same time, there is a hunger for spiritual reality and a different style of life – to be seen in the interest in meditation, yoga and new forms of religious life. Many people with no religious allegiance have a deep concern for the future of the planet, shown in the willingness to raise money for the starving and in the rapid growth of interest in ecological concerns. Modern communication, human migration and opportunities for travel are creating an international society – even if it is also marked by new emphasis on regional and ethnic identity.

There are those who speak in almost apocalyptic terms of growing rivalry between Christendom and the Islamic world, and some societies are split by communalism, which is often fuelled by religious differences. The alternative to increasing competition is co-operation, and this implies some shared values. The search for a global ethic is a necessary part of the search for lasting peace and for the survival of the planet. It can be seen therefore as directly relevant to young people and the sort of world in which they grow up.

If this search starts from Hans Küng's *Humanum*, it is one in which people of every religion and culture can take part. The essential question, in Küng's words, is 'What is good for human beings?' It is a question of immediate relevance on which everyone may be expected to have an opinion. Obviously answers will differ – even within one church there can be sharp disagreements, for example, about attitudes to birth control, abortion or homosexuality. There are differences about whether the use of force is ever right, and if so when. But the disagreements can be seen as different ways of trying to reach the same goal. The answer to the question 'What is good for human beings' is one that every person can attempt to answer. Those answers may then be compared with and corrected by the answers of other people and of the great spiritual teachers of the past. Such an approach may allow one to rediscover the ethical teachings of the great religions as a rich resource rather than an oppressive authority. This would be in line with an experiential approach to teaching.

The documents reproduced below can be seen as attempts by various members of the world religions to answer the question 'What is good for human beings?' – even if that is not how the question was formulated. They provide material against which young people and all who are concerned for the future of the planet can compare their own insights and share in the task of discovering a global ethic. For whilst this ethic will be enriched by the heritage offered by the world religions, to be effective it will need to be discovered and owned by the people of today's world.

The horrors of this century, with its wars, with its death camps, with its sophisticated torture and its apparent indifference to the starvation of millions, remind us how fragile is the ethical veneer of civilized society. Chaos is never far away. A global ethic would help people to recognize that there are certain norms of behaviour which are universally valid and strengthen the individual's will to resist inhumane orders. The recognition of universal human rights implies the recognition of universal obligations. The question 'what is good for human beings?' is about not only what is good for us but what is good for others. It may perhaps not be surprising that at the heart of the global ethic will be the Golden Rule – to be found in every religion – 'Do unto others as you would have them do unto you'. The challenge is to work out the implications for a world society in terms of both individual and corporate behaviour.

A world society needs a global ethic. To its articulation people of every faith have a rich contribution to make. The documents reproduced below are an indication of the progress already made by some people of faith who have met together. They are a resource for future work.

PART II

I

The Universal Declaration of Human Rights

This was adopted by the General Assembly of the United Nations on 10 December 1948. Although not a religious document, it was influenced by some religious groups[1] and provides a standard of comparison for subsequent documents.

Universal Declaration of Human Rights
Adopted by the General Assembly of the United Nations
10 December 1948

Preamble

Whereas recognition of the inherent dignity and of the equal and inalienable rights of all members of the human family is the foundation of freedom, justice and peace in the world,

Whereas disregard and contempt for human rights have resulted in barbarous acts which have outraged the conscience of mankind, and the advent of a world in which human beings shall enjoy freedom of speech and belief and freedom from fear and want has been proclaimed as the highest aspiration of the common people,

Whereas it is essential, if man is not to be compelled to have recourse, as a last resort, to rebellion against tyranny and oppression, that human rights should be protected by the rule of law,

Whereas it is essential to promote the development of friendly relations between nations,

Whereas the peoples of the United Nations have in the Charter reaffirmed their faith in fundamental human rights, in the dignity and worth of the human person and in the equal rights of men and women and have determined to promote social progress and better standards of life in larger freedom,

Whereas Member States have pledged themselves to achieve, in cooperation with the United Nations, the promotion of universal respect for and observance of human rights and fundamental freedoms,

Whereas a common understanding of these rights and freedoms is of the greatest importance for the full realization of this pledge.

Now, Therefore,

The General Assembly
proclaims

This universal declaration of human rights as a common standard of achievement for all peoples and all nations, to the end that every individual and every organ of society, keeping this Declaration constantly in mind, shall strive by teaching and education to promote respect for these rights and freedoms and by progressive measures, national and international, to secure their universal and effective recognition and observance, both among the peoples of Member States themselves and among the peoples of territories under their jurisdiction.

Article 1

All human beings are born free and equal in dignity and rights. They are endowed with reason and conscience and should act towards one another in a spirit of brotherhood.

Article 2

Everyone is entitled to all the rights and freedoms set forth in this Declaration, without distinction of any kind, such as race, colour, sex, language, religion, political or other opinion, national or social origin, property, birth or other status.
Furthermore, no distinction shall be made on the basis of the political, jurisdictional or international status of the country or territory to which a person belongs, whether it be independent, trust, non-self-governing or under any other limitation of sovereignty.

Article 3

Everyone has the right to life, liberty and security of person.

Article 4

No one shall be held in slavery or servitude; slavery and the slave trade shall be prohibited in all their forms.

Article 5

No one shall be subjected to torture or to cruel, inhuman or degrading treatment or punishment.

Article 6

Everyone has the right to recognition everywhere as a person before the law.

Article 7

All are equal before the law and are entitled without any discrimination to equal protection of the law. All are entitled to equal protection against any discrimination in violation of this Declaration and against any incitement to such discrimination.

Article 8

Everyone has the right to an effective remedy by the competent national tribunals for acts violating the fundamental rights granted him by the constitution or by law.

Article 9

No one shall be subjected to arbitrary arrest, detention or exile.

Article 10

Everyone is entitled in full equality to a fair and public hearing by an independent and impartial tribunal, in the determination of his rights and obligations and of any criminal charge against him.

Article 11

1. Everyone charged with a penal offence has the right to be presumed innocent until proved guilty according to law in a public trial at which he has had all the guarantees necessary for his defence.
2. No one shall be held guilty of any penal offence on account of any act or omission which did not constitute a penal offence, under national or international law, at the time when it was committed. Nor shall a heavier penalty be imposed than the one that was applicable at the time the penal offence was committed.

Article 12

No one shall be subjected to arbitrary interference with his privacy, family, home or correspondence, nor to attacks upon his honour and reputation. Everyone has the right to the protection of the law against such interference or attacks.

Article 13

1. Everyone has the right to freedom of movement and residence within the borders of each state.
2. Everyone has the right to leave any country, including his own, and to return to his country.

Article 14

1. Everyone has the right to seek and to enjoy in other countries asylum from persecution.
2. This right may not be invoked in the case of prosecutions genuinely arising from non-political crimes or from acts contrary to the purposes and principles of the United Nations.

Article 15

1. Everyone has the right to a nationality.
2. No one shall be arbitrarily deprived of his nationality nor denied the right to change his nationality.

Article 16

1. Men and women of full age, without any limitation due to race, nationality or religion, have the right to marry and to found a family. They are entitled to equal rights as to marriage, during marriage and at its dissolution.
2. Marriage shall be entered into only with the free and full consent of the intending spouses.
3. The family is the natural and fundamental group unit of society and is entitled to protection by society and the State.

Article 17

1. Everyone has the right to own property alone as well as in association with others.
2. No one shall be arbitrarily deprived of his property.

Article 18

Everyone has the right to freedom of thought, conscience and religion; this right includes freedom to change his religion or belief, and freedom, either alone or in community with others and in public or private, to manifest his religion or belief in teaching, practice, worship and observance.

Article 19

Everyone has the right to freedom of opinion and expression; this right includes freedom to hold opinions without interference and to seek, receive and impart information and ideas through any media and regardless of frontiers.

Article 20

1. Everyone has the right to freedom of peaceful assembly and association.
2. No one may be compelled to belong to an association.

Article 21

1. Everyone has the right to take part in the government of his country, directly or through freely chosen representatives.
2. Everyone has the right of equal access to public service in his country.
3. The will of the people shall be the basis of the authority of government; this will shall be expressed in periodic and genuine elections which shall be by universal and equal suffrage and shall be held by secret vote or by equivalent free voting procedures.

Article 22

Everyone, as a member of society, has the right to social security and is entitled to realization, through national effort and international co-operation and in accordance with the organization and resources of each State, of the economic, social and cultural rights indispensable for his dignity and the free development of his personality.

Article 23

1. Everyone has the right to work, to free choice of employment, to just and favourable conditions of work and to protection against unemployment.
2. Everyone, without any discrimination, has the right to equal pay for equal work.
3. Everyone who works has the right to just and favourable remuneration ensuring for himself and his family an existence worthy of human dignity, and supplemented, if necessary, by other means of social protection.
4. Everyone has the right to form and to join trade unions for the protection of his interests.

Article 24

Everyone has the right to rest and leisure, including reasonable limitation of working hours and periodic holidays with pay.

Article 25

1. Everyone has the right to a standard of living adequate for the health and

well-being of himself and of his family, including food, clothing, housing
and medical care and necessary social services, and the right to security in
the event of unemployment, sickness, disability, widowhood, old age or
other lack of livelihood in circumstances beyond his control.

2. Motherhood and childhood are entitled to special care and assistance. All
children, whether born in or out of wedlock, shall enjoy the same social
protection.

Article 26

1. Everyone has the right to education. Education shall be free, at least in the
elementary and fundamental stages. Elementary education shall be
compulsory. Technical and professional education shall be made generally
available and higher education shall be equally accessible to all on the basis
of merit.

2. Education shall be directed to the full development of the human
personality and to the strengthening of respect for human rights and
fundamental freedoms. It shall promote understanding, tolerance and
friendship among all nations, racial or religious groups, and shall further
the activities of the United Nations for the maintenance of peace.

3. Parents have a prior right to choose the kind of education that shall be given
to their children.

Article 27

1. Everyone has the right freely to participate in the cultural life of the
community, to enjoy the arts and to share in scientific advancement and its
benefits.

2. Everyone has the right to the protection of the moral and material interests
resulting from any scientific, literary or artistic production of which he is
the author.

Article 28

Everyone is entitled to a social and international order in which the rights and
freedoms set forth in this Declaration can be fully realized.

Article 29

1. Everyone has duties to the community in which alone the free and full
development of his personality is possible.

2. In the exercise of his rights and freedoms, everyone shall be subject only to
such limitations as are determined by law solely for the purpose of securing
due recognition and respect for the rights and freedoms of others and of

meeting the just requirements of morality, public order and the general welfare in a democratic society.

3. These rights and freedoms may in no case be exercised contrary to the purposes and principles of the United Nations.

Article 30

Nothing in this Declaration may be interpreted as implying for any State, group or person any right to engage in any activity or to perform any act aimed at the destruction of any of the rights and freedoms set forth herein.

Declaration on the Elimination of All Forms of Intolerance and of Discrimination Based on Religion or Belief

This was adopted by the General Assembly of the United Nations on 25 November 1981. Work on this declaration took nearly twenty years, but the long discussions themselves focussed attention on the widespread practice of religious discrimination. Non Governmental Organizations (NGOs) played a persistent part in gaining support for the Declaration. In March 1981 the drafting was suddenly completed by a Working Group and adopted by the parent Commission with only five socialist states abstaining.[1]

Declaration on the Elimination of All Forms of Intolerance and of Discrimination Based on Religion or Belief

(Adopted by the General Assembly of the United Nations, 25 November 1981)

The General Assembly,

Considering that one of the basic principles of the Charter of the United Nations is that of the dignity and equality inherent in all human beings, and that all Member States have pledged themselves to take joint and separate action in cooperation with the Organization to promote and encourage universal respect for and observance of human rights and fundamental freedoms for all, without distinction as to race, sex, language, or religion,

Considering that the Universal Declaration of Human Rights and the International Covenants on Human Rights proclaim the principles of nondiscrimination and equality before the law and the right to freedom of thought, conscience, religion, and belief,

Considering that the disregard and infringement of human rights and fundamental freedoms, in particular of the right to freedom of thought, conscience, religion, or whatever belief, have brought, directly or indirectly, wars and great suffering to [hu]mankind,[2] especially where they serve as a means of foreign interference in the internal affairs of other States and amount to kindling hatred between peoples and nations,

Considering that religion or belief, for anyone who professes either, is one of the fundamental elements in [one's] conception of life and that freedom of religion or belief should be fully respected and guaranteed,

Considering that it is essential to promote understanding, tolerance, and respect in matters relating to freedom of religion and belief and to ensure that the use of religion or belief for ends inconsistent with the Charter, other relevant instruments of the United Nations, and the purposes and principles of the present Declaration is inadmissible,

Convinced that freedom of religion and belief should also contribute to the attainment of the goals of world peace, social justice and friendship among peoples and to the elimination of ideologies or practices of colonialism and racial discrimination,

Noting with satisfaction the adoption of several, and the coming into force of some, conventions, under the aegis of the United Nations and of the specialized agencies, for the elimination of various forms of discrimination,

Concerned by manifestations of intolerance and by the existence of discrimination in matters of religion or belief still in evidence in some areas of the world,

Resolved to adopt all necessary measures for the speedy elimination of such intolerance in all its forms and manifestations and to prevent and combat discrimination on the grounds of religion or belief,

Proclaims this Declaration on the Elimination of All Forms of Intolerance and of Discrimination Based on Religion or Belief:

Article 1

1. Everyone shall have the right to freedom of thought, conscience, and religion. This right shall include freedom to have a religion or whatever belief of [one's] choice, and freedom, either individually or in community with others and in public or private, to manifest [one's] religion or belief in worship, observance, practice, and teaching.
2. No one shall be subject to coercion which would impair [one's] freedom to have a religion or belief of [one's] choice.
3. Freedom to manifest one's religion or beliefs may be subject only to such limitations as are prescribed by law and are necessary to protect public safety, order, health, or morals or the fundamental rights and freedoms of others.

Article 2

1. No one shall be subject to discrimination by any State, institution, group of persons, or person on the grounds of religion or other beliefs.
2. For the purposes of the present Declaration, the expression 'intolerance and discrimination based on religion or belief' means any distinction, exclusion, restriction, or preference based on religion or belief and having as its purpose or as its effect nullification or impairment of the recognition, enjoyment, or exercise of human rights and fundamental freedoms on an equal basis.

Article 3

Discrimination between human beings on the grounds of religion or belief constitutes an affront to human dignity and a disavowal of the principles of the Charter of the United Nations, and shall be condemned as a violation of the human rights and fundamental freedoms proclaimed in the Universal Declaration of Human Rights and enunciated in detail in the International Covenants on Human Rights, and as an obstacle to friendly and peaceful relations between nations.

Article 4

1. All States shall take effective measures to prevent and eliminate discrimination on the grounds of religion or belief in the recognition, exercise, and enjoyment of human rights and fundamental freedoms in all fields of civil, economic, political, social and cultural life.
2. All States shall make all efforts to enact or rescind legislation where necessary to prohibit any such discrimination, and to take all appropriate measures to combat intolerance on the grounds of religion or other beliefs in this matter.

Article 5

1. The parents or, as the case may be, the legal guardians of the child have the right to organize the life within the family in accordance with their religion or belief and bearing in mind the moral education in which they believe the child should be brought up.
2. Every child shall enjoy the right to have access to education in the matter of religion or belief in accordance with the wishes of his [or her] parents or, as the case may be, legal guardians, and shall not be compelled to receive teaching on religion or belief against the wishes of his [or her] parents or legal guardians, the best interests of the child being the guiding principle.
3. The child shall be protected from any form of discrimination on the grounds of religion or belief. He [or she] shall be brought up in a spirit of

understanding, tolerance, friendship among peoples, peace and universal brother[sister]hood, respect for freedom of religion or belief of others, and in full consciousness that his [or her] energy and talents should be devoted to the service of his [or her] fellow [human beings].

4. In the case of a child who is not under the care either of his [or her] parents or legal guardians, due account shall be taken of their expressed wishes or of any other proof of their wishes in the matter of religion or belief, the best interests of the child being the guiding principle.

5. Practices of a religion or beliefs in which a child is brought up must not be injurious to his [or her] physical health or to his [or her] full development, taking into account article 1, paragraph 3, of the present Declaration.

Article 6

In accordance with article 1 of the present Declaration, and subject to the provisions of article 1, paragraph 3, the right to freedom of thought, conscience, religion, or belief shall include, *inter alia*, the following freedoms:

(a) to worship or assemble in connection with a religion or belief, and to establish and maintain places for these purposes;

(b) to establish and maintain appropriate charitable or humanitarian institutions;

(c) to make, acquire, and use to an adequate extent the necessary articles and materials related to the rites or customs of a religion or belief;

(d) to write, issue, and disseminate relevant publications in these areas;

(e) to teach a religion or belief in places suitable for these purposes;

(f) to solicit and receive voluntary financial and other contributions from individuals and institutions;

(g) to train, appoint, elect, or designate by succession appropriate leaders called for by the requirements and standards of any religion or belief;

(h) to observe days of rest and to celebrate holidays and ceremonies in accordance with the precepts of one's religion or belief;

(i) to establish and maintain communications with individuals and communities in matters of religion and belief at the national and international levels.

Article 7

The rights and freedoms set forth in the present Declaration shall be accorded in national legislations in such a manner that everyone shall be able to avail him [or her] self of such rights and freedoms in practice.

Article 8

Nothing in the present Declaration shall be construed as restricting or derogating from any right defined in the Universal Declaration of Human Rights and the International Covenants on Human Rights.

3

Fundamental Postulates of Christianity and Judaism in Relation to Human Order

In August 1946, surprisingly soon after the end of the Second World War, some 100 Christians and Jews from 15 countries met at Lady Margaret Hall, Oxford. The theme of the Conference was 'Freedom, Justice and Responsibility'. There were six commissions. The second commission agreed a declaration on 'Fundamental Postulates of Judaism and Christianity in Relation to the Social Order' which is reproduced below. It is particularly interesting to see a concern at this early date for a right use of natural resources.

Findings of Commission No.2 of the International Conference of Christians and Jews, Oxford, 1946

As Christians and Jews, while recognizing the important religious differences between us, we affirm on the basis of divine revelation that the dignity, rights and duties of man derive from his creation by God and his relation to God.

We acknowledge God as the Creator and Lord of the universe, and as the Father of all human beings: we see in their relation to God the bond which unites them even amid division and conflict, and in Him the authority to which all are subject. Moreover, we find the basic motive for ethical conduct in man's response to God as he makes Himself known in His wisdom and goodness.

By the will of God in creation man is both an individual and a member of society, so that both individuals and communities owe obedience to His rule. Moreover, there is true community only where there is full personal life, and vice versa.

Therefore:

We acknowledge the authority of the moral principles which are implicit in the nature of man in virtue of his relation to God and of his qualities as a rational, moral and social being. From these it follows that it is the duty of men to respect in others the right to:

1. LIFE. Since each human being is the child of God and has special

value in His sight as an individual, his life must be respected and preserved. At the same time, he must similarly respect the life of his fellow-men and is under obligation to promote his good.

2. LIBERTY.   The responsibility which falls upon man as a child and servant of God involves the necessity for freedom. He must, therefore, be given opportunity for the free exercise of the spiritual and moral powers entrusted to him. Life in organized society makes demands and entails restrictions upon the individual, but the fundamental principles of liberty alike for the individual and communities may never be sacrificed.

3. PERSONAL DIGNITY.   Each individual possesses worth as a person and must treat others as such, while other persons and the community must accord similar treatment to him. This principle involves recognition of his status as a member of society with a contribution to make to the whole, and is opposed to discrimination on grounds of colour, race or creed.

We repudiate both the individualism which would make a man a law unto himself and the totalitarianism which would subordinate and sacrifice all other values to race, nation, state, class or party. Against the first, we claim that only as a man accepts himself from God and all his life as under God can he truly live. Against the second we affirm that all human institutions stand under God's rule and judgment and that none may usurp the loyalty which is due to Him Alone.

Rights are exercised and duties discharged in a world which includes things as well as persons. Here we would maintain the following principles:

1. Things must be subordinated to persons, and property rights should always be secondary to consideration of human welfare and social justice.

2. Nature is to be respected and not merely exploited. It is a revelation of God and a sphere of His purpose: man may not squander its bounty and must show due regard for its beauty.

The right attitude of a community to its members, of persons to persons, and of persons to things, cannot be fully achieved without the recognition, alike by the individual and by the community, of God and of the relation of man and nature to Him. Corporate recognition of God will include, in addition to the moral obligations of society, all that comes within the compass of worship.

Divided as we are in the forms of public worship, we are united in affirming the value of it and the need to participate in it if a right human order is to be achieved. Religious communities have therefore the right to exist and also the right to their own freedom of activity. Without the recognition of this right the political community is impoverished.

The moral law which is rooted in God and implanted in man's nature is binding, not only upon individuals, but also upon society in all its groupings.

1. Within the state there should be respect for the family, freedom for a rich and varied group-life; above the state is the will of God as manifest in the universal moral law.

2. Society is preeminently the sphere of justice, by which the relationships between individuals are so ordered that each may perform his duties and be assured of his rights. This can be achieved only under some form of government which recognizes the social, political and religious rights and responsibilities of individuals and groups.
3. Society is equally under an obligation to use all its resources for the welfare of all its members. That implies education, adequate provision against want, opportunity of service and conditions which will enable every individual to be at home in the community and every community to be at home in the larger human society.

Man's recognition of himself and of his neighbour as children of God should issue in a charity and righteousness which, while but imperfectly embodied in the forms and laws of organised society, work constantly to transform them into an ever more adequate expression. We therefore, Christians and Jews alike, call upon all who share the religious convictions and the ethical standards here set out to cooperate for the realization of this ideal.

4

Declarations of the World Conference on Religion and Peace

The World Conference on Religion and Peace held its first Assembly at Kyoto, Japan, in October 1970. It has held four subsequent assemblies. Its concerns have tended to parallel those of the United Nations, with an emphasis on the need for disarmament, development, protection of human rights and increasingly on preservation of the environment. WCRP's membership is drawn from every religion and from most countries of the world. Great care is madè to balance participation to try to ensure that assemblies are representative, although most participants come in an individual capacity rather than as a delegate.

The Declarations are approved by the whole Assembly, whereas Commission reports are approved by members of the Commission and received by the Assembly.

THE WORLD CONFERENCE ON RELIGION AND PEACE

I

The First Assembly
Kyoto, Japan
16–21 October 1970

1. The Kyoto Declaration
2. Report on Disarmament (Extracts)
3. Report on Development (Extracts)
4. Report on Human Rights (Extracts)
5. Other Resolutions of the Conference (Extracts)

The full proceedings of the Kyoto Conference are published in *Religion for Peace*, ed. Homer A. Jack, Gandhi Peace Foundation, New Delhi and Bharatiya Vidya Bharan, Bombay 1973.

1. The Kyoto Declaration, October 1970

The World Conference on Religion and Peace represents an historic attempt to bring together men and women of all major religions to discuss the urgent issue of peace. We meet at a crucial time. At this very moment we are faced by cruel and inhuman wars and by racial, social, and economic violence. Man's continued existence on this planet is threatened with nuclear extinction. Never has there been such despair among men. Our deep conviction that the religions of the world have a real and important service to render the cause of peace has brought us to Kyoto from the four corners of the earth. Baha'i, Buddhist, Confucian, Christian, Hindu, Jain, Jew, Muslim, Shintoist, Sikh, Zoroastrian, and others – we have come together in peace out of a common concern for peace.

As we sat down together facing the overriding issues of peace we discovered that the things which unite us are more important than the things which divide us. We found that we share:

A conviction of the fundamental unity of the human family, and the equality and dignity of all human beings;

A sense of the sacredness of the individual person and his conscience;

A sense of the value of human community;

A realization that might is not right; that human power is not self-sufficient and absolute;

A belief that love, compassion, selflessness, and the force of inner truthfulness and of the spirit have ultimately greater power than hate, enmity, and self-interest;

A sense of obligation to stand on the side of the poor and the oppressed as against the rich and the oppressors; and

A profound hope that good will finally prevail.

Because of these convictions that we hold in common, we believe that a special charge has been given to all men and women of religion to be concerned with all their hearts and minds with peace and peace-making, to be the servants of peace. As men and women of religion we confess in humility and penitence that we have very often betrayed our religious ideals and our commitment to peace. It is not religion that has failed the cause of peace, but religious people. This betrayal of religion can and must be corrected.

In confronting the urgent challenges to peace in the second half of the twentieth century, we were compelled to consider the problems of disarmament, development, and human rights. Clearly, peace is imperilled by the ever-quickening race for armaments, the widening gap between the rich and the poor within and among the nations, and by the tragic violation of human rights all over the world. In our consideration of the problems of disarmament we became convinced that peace cannot be found through the stockpiling of weapons. We therefore call for immediate steps toward general disarmament, to include all weapons of destruction – conventional, nuclear, chemical, and biological. We found that the problems of development were aggravated by the fact that the resources spent on research, and on the manufacture and stock-piling of such weapons, consumes a grossly inordinate amount of the resources of mankind. We are convinced that these resources are urgently needed instead to combat the injustices that make for war and other forms of social violence. Any society in which one out of every four children dies is in a state of war. While development, of itself, may not bring peace, there can be no lasting peace without it. Therefore, we pledge our support to the effort of the United Nations to make the 1970s a decade of development for all mankind.

The social convulsions clearly evident in the world today demonstrate the connection between peace and the recognition, promotion, and protection of human rights. Racial discrimination, the repression of ethnic and religious minorities, the torturing of political and other prisoners, legalized and *de-facto* denial of political freedom and equality of opportunity, the denial of equal rights to women, any form of colonialist oppression – all such violations of human rights are responsible for the escalation of violence that is debasing human civilization.

While we of this Conference speak for ourselves as persons brought together from many religions by our deep concern for peace, we try also to speak for the vast majority of the human family who are powerless and whose voice is seldom heard – the poor, the exploited, the refugees, and all who are homeless and whose lives, fields, and freedoms have been devastated by wars. We speak to our religions, the ecumenical councils and all inter-faith effort for peace, to the nations, beginning with our own, to the United Nations, and to men and women outside established religions who are concerned about human welfare.

To one and all, beginning with ourselves, we say that the point of departure for any serious effort in the human enterprise – educational, cultural, scientific, social, and religious – is the solemn acceptance of the fact that men and all their works are now united in one destiny. We live or die together; we can continue to drift toward a common doom or we can engage together in the struggle for peace. We cannot honestly denounce war and the things that make for war unless our personal lives are informed by peace and we are prepared to make the necessary sacrifices for it. We must do all in our power to educate public opinion and awaken public conscience to take a firm stand against war and the illusory hope of peace though military victory. We are convinced that religions, in spite of historic differences, must now seek to unite all men in those endeavours which make for true peace. We believe that we have a duty transcending sectarian limits to cooperate with those outside the historic religions who share our desire for peace.

We pledge ourselves to warn the nations whose citizens we are that the effort to achieve and maintain military power is the road to disaster. It creates a climate of fear and mistrust; it demands resources needed for the meeting of the needs of health, housing, and welfare; it fosters the escalation of the arms race that now threatens man's life on earth; it sharpens differences among nations into military and economic blocs; it regards peace as an armed truce or a balance of terror; it dismisses as utopian a truly universal concern for the welfare of all mankind. To all this we say 'No!'

We desire to convey our concern for peace to the United Nations. The achievement and maintenance of peace requires not only a recognition of the existence of the United Nations but, even more, support for and implementation of its decisions. We urge universal membership in the United Nations, a more just sharing of power and responsibility in its procedures. We urge the member-nations to accept its leadership in resolving issues that have led or may lead to conflicts.

It is our hope that this Conference will help us see and accept our responsibility as men and women of religious faith for the achievement of true and lasting peace.

Conference Message Committee

Dr Harold A. Bosley (convenor and chairman), Dr Ralph D. Abernathy, Miss Elisabeth Adler, Dr Manzoor Ahmad, Mrs Anna Bennett, Mr Alexey

Bouevsky, Canon Burgess Carr, Prof Max Charlesworth, Sri Shankarrao Deo, Rev Kando Enishi, Prof Yoskiaki Iisaka, Rev Michisuke Kawashima, Father Theophane Mathias, Mrs Bagos Oka, and Rabbi W. Gunther Plaut.

2. Disarmament

The report sees in the build up of arms 'a threat to world peace, a hindrance to development and a mockery of human rights' (p. 161). Rejecting the view that fear of military retaliation is the best guarantee of peace, it lists various steps which could be taken to reduce the threat of war. It calls for a reduction in the arms trade.

The link between disarmament and development is stressed. Governments of the world spend three times as much on the means of destruction as on public health. The expenditure on arms by developing countries distorts their economies. The practical concern of religions with all aspects of life is recognized.

The Approach

The report rejects the view 'that fear of military retaliation is a positive deterrent to war and that therefore it is the best guarantee of world peace. We hold that arms will drive the world to a clash of arms and that the stockpiling of the means of mass destruction produces fears and creates a war psychosis which may trigger off a violent struggle . . . Peace is a prerequisite of development' (p. 162).

The Recommendations

1*. 'We wish to declare ourselves as religionists: (a) in favour of all steps towards the prevention of nuclear proliferation; (b) in favour of associating the People's Republic of China and France with the international agreements and ongoing talks about nuclear disarmament; (c) against the development, manufacture, or use of all bacteriological, chemical and biological agents of mass destruction; (d) for conducting research into methods of destroying stockpiles without harming nature; (e) for putting an end to all nuclear tests, including underground tests for destructive puposes; (f) against the use of the sea bed and oceans for the development of new weapons and in particular nuclear weapons; (g) for continuing discussion between the USA and the USSR about the limitation of strategic arms; and (h) for the creation of nuclear-free zones' (p. 163).

5. The dangers of the arms trade are recognized

'We believe that the sale of arms, mostly by wealthy nations, constitutes a

* Numbers refer to the numbers of the recommendations.

danger to peace, that it is a subtle form of colonialism misdirecting to wasteful and destructive ends resources that could assist the developing countries. Therefore, we call urgently for the institution of measures to register, control, and bring to an end the international trade in arms both by governments and private agencies, and as a first step we ask the United Nations to institute and publish a world register of arms sales' (pp. 163–4).

6. *The link between disarmament and development is again stressed*

'We are convinced that there is a close and direct relation between disarmament and development. Hence we press governments seriously to consider their national priorities and to see whether in all conscience they are exercising responsible stewardship of their resources. We believe that aid from developed to developing countries should preclude military aid and should ensure that economic aid given does not enable them to divert their own resources to increase their military expenditures' (p. 164).

7. *The way of non-violence is commended*

'We religionists further believe that disarmament must be accompanied by a resolve to adhere to non-violence as an individual way of life, and as a means to resolve conflicts and that steps need to be taken to institute machinery for resolving conflicts, both national and international, through non-violent means and peaceful negotiations.'

12. *Religion's failure at times to be involved with all life is recognized*

'We recognize, as religionists, the fact that organized religion and its leaders have not always practised nor understood that religion is vitally concerned with all aspects of life – including political, social, and economic – and have tended to compartmentalize life into spiritual and material, promoting an unconcern for the latter' (p. 165).

3. Development (pp. 167–174)

This report again emphasizes the link between development and peace. It warns of the dangers of pollution, not yet out of concern for nature in its own right, but because of its adverse effect on human life. Continuing 'neo-colonial' exploitation is recognized. It says that religions should be penitent for the past but are now agreed in shaping the future. It suggests there should be various models for development. Social justice should take priority over economic growth. The importance of education is stressed. Aid by religious bodies should not be motivated by self-interest.

Development is the 'new name for peace'

'Peace is a dynamic process creating order with justice. A society in which millions of human beings are subjected to oppressive economic, social, or political conditions, which condemn them to a haunted life of misery, to a level of marginal existence unfit for human beings, is not a just society and, therefore, is not at peace. It is in a state of constant war. It is in this sense that development may be said to be the "new name for peace". And it is in this sense that the problem of peace cannot be separated from the problem of development' (p. 167).

Dangers of Pollution

'Man has proved his ability to produce wealth. He has yet to demonstrate his ability to use it for the good of man. With it and for the sake of it, he fouls his rivers, poisons his lakes, contaminates the oceans, pollutes the atmosphere' (p. 167).

Continuing Exploitation

'Eighty per cent of the world's goods are in the hands of a small minority of the world's people and the gap between rich and poor individuals and nations grows constantly wider. This solution is a consequence of colonialism. If for the most part the colonial empires have disappeared, the economic shackles forged are not so easily broken. Most of the new nations remain producers of raw materials, subjected to the vicissitudes of a world market of which the terms of trade are not in their favour, and are blocked by the restrictive tariff policies of the powerful industralized nations from developing export industries of their own' (pp. 167–8).

Repentance

'What should be the attitude of religion in the face of these realities? Its first posture should be one of repentance for having remained singularly indifferent to the idolatry of riches and the perversion of their use. Especially called to penance is the Christian world inasmuch as, with some exceptions, the part of the world where wealth is concentrated is – or is called – Christian. Contrary to the spirit of Christ, social justice was protected by the paradoxical attitude of many Christians who looked upon the accumulation of wealth as a reward for virtue and the burden of poverty as a punishment for sin or a cross to be borne in expectation of liberation in the next world. Religions other than Christian are, however, not to be entirely absolved of blame. For, by their excessive emphasis upon the relative unimportance of the material, they weakened the forces opposed to its hegemony' (p. 168).

'Man participates in the creation of his own history'

Today, the major religions of the world agree that man participates in the creation of his own history. He is not the helpless pawn of blind forces. This is why we repent for the present situation and at the same time hope for the future. We believe that men can be transformed. We also believe that the political, economic, social, and even religious institutions created by man are no less in need of transformation. They must be radically changed. In making the liberation of man from poverty, ignorance, war and other forms of oppression a matter of central concern, the religions are not abandoning their principles but renewing their basic understanding and traditions. The basic values of respect and reverence for life, compassion, love, and the brotherhood of man are common to all religions.

The basic values of the ancient religious traditions are in no way opposed to development. On the contrary, however, over the long centuries, customs and traditions, many of which are impediments to human progress, have like barnacles attached themselves to all religions without exception. Because of this many of the younger generation today reject traditional values entirely. They regard them as obstacles to change and the effort to preserve them as in fact contributing to the preservation of the status quo. They argue, sometimes angrily, that new values must be sought without regard for the past. It is, however, impossible to destroy cultures and value systems which have lasted for hundreds of years. Even were it possible, what would emerge from the ruins would be a twentieth century barbarian without cultural roots. What is imperative, therefore, is not the total rejection of traditional values, but an honest and critical examination of them to separate the essential from the accretions of time. The former which can serve to further the development of man should be preserved, renewed and strengthened. The latter, which stand in the way, must be courageously removed' (p. 169).

Various Models

'We reject the notion that the industrialized nations supply the "model" of development' (p. 170).

'There is no universal model of development. Each country must establish and be free to establish its own model' (p. 171).

Social Justice

'In searching for solutions to the problem, priority must be given to social justice over economic growth' (p. 172).

Education for Development

'Nothing is more important to development than education. The richer people must be educated to understand the unity of mankind, the requirements of justice, and their responsibility to achieve it. In the developing world education must awaken in the masses an awareness of their dignity and of their rights. They must be made to realize that the goods of the world were created for the benefit of all and that they have an inalienable right to share, which they must assert.

Education for development in the developing world involves eradication of illiteracy; changing certain attitudes not corresponding to the needs of the times regarding work and human dignity; helping to distinguish between basic values and peripheral traditions; producing a civic sense, social conscience, and national commitment; developing motivation; and stimulating a capacity for personal and independent thinking. Religion should play a major role in developing the moral and spiritual resources of man which are of the highest importance. Religious education should be given in the schools in their own respective religions by their own respective teachers, while in the universities, comparative religion should be part of the curriculum.'

'The role of women must be stressed and educational programmes planned which will enable them to realize their potentialities. If women are not liberated from the discrimination which inhibits their full participation, development will fail.'

Aid should not be self-interested

'To use aid for the purpose of proselytizing is offensive to believers in other religions . . . We recommend that religious people should broaden their commitment by a readiness to cooperate with all agencies and individuals who are working to humanize society whether they are of the same religion, of other religions, or of none' (p. 173).

4. Human Rights (pp. 175–184)

The fundamental relationship between peace and human rights is recognized. The importance of human rights is based in the appreciation of the worth of the human person which is found in all religions.

The report draws attention to the evils of torture, of modern warfare and of racism. It warns of the threats to minorities, to cultural diversification, to religious liberty and to the rights of conscientious objectors and of women. It stresses the need for machinery to investigate abuses of human rights and the importance of education. In recognizing the right to resist oppression, the report strongly recommends the use of non-violent means.

Peace and Human Rights

'There is a fundamental relationship between peace and human rights. The effective protection of human dignity and of the rights of human beings is an essential requirement for a peaceful world. The meaning and importance of human rights will be found only on the basis of a true appreciation of the worth of the human person; this is accepted, although perhaps expressed in different terms, by all religions. It must at the same time be pointed out that religions in their historical manifestations have not always been respectful of human rights themselves and have on some occasions purported to justify violations of human rights on religious grounds. This makes it all the more urgent that religions should be sensitized to the vital necessity of promoting and protecting human rights. This is necessary not only as a basis for lasting peace but also as a foundation for social justice' (p. 175).

'In order to restore credence in the moral and ethical authority of religion, the religious leaders of the world will have to take much more active and positive leadership in a continuous effort for creating effective awareness of human rights and their promotion at all levels' (p. 176).

Torture and the Cruelty of War

'The torture and ill treatment of prisoners which is carried out with the authority of some governments constitute not only a crime against humanity but also a crime against the moral laws.

The use of napalm, defoliants, and other deadly chemicals, the massacres of prisoners and civilians, and the aerial bombardment of defenceless towns and villages are not only crimes against humanity but offences against the moral law. Yet, these monstrous crimes occur daily in our midst on the authority of governments which claim to be law-abiding and respectful of the moral law. Thus, the bad example given by some governments is the cause of the general increase and competition in violence throughout the world. If governments themselves do not respect the sacredness of human life and the dignity of human beings, it is likely that those who consider themselves victims of injustices will follow the example given to them by governments.

In this grave situation the leaders of religions should not hesitate to denounce fearlessly and consistently brutality and violations of the laws of humanity. In addition, religions should urge the adoption, at national and international levels, of measures to put a stop to the brutalization of mankind' (p. 176).

Protection of Human Rights

'At present, there is no international body authorized to investigate such violations; therefore, governments are free to violate the humanitarian laws with complete immunity from even the criticism of the United Nations and world public opinion. This Conference, therefore, urges as a matter of urgency, the establishment, within the framework of the UN, of a permanent and objective Commission of Inquiry empowered to investigate all violations of humanitarian conventions in the armed conflicts which disgrace this era. This UN Commission of Inquiry should report publicly to the Security Council and to the General Assembly. Thus the sanction of at least the United Nations and of world public opinion might deter governments from violations of the humanitarian laws.

Generally speaking, it is at the domestic level that human rights can most effectively be protected. The representatives of religions should use actively their influence in each country to secure the application of the principles of the Universal Declaration in national laws' (p. 177).

Education

'In order to ensure the more effective protection of human rights it is urged that religions should promote an active educational campaign to ensure a fuller knowledge of the provisions of the Universal Declaration of Human Rights and subsequent instruments for the protection of human rights and the elimination of racialism. Such an educational programme should be undertaken at all levels and through all the educational institutions. The aim of such education should be to inspire respect for the dignity of each human being.

Particular attention should be given to the teaching of human rights to adult populations. For this purpose, special efforts should be made to ensure that full use is made of the mass media and also that books and pamphlets are published and distributed through religious organizations.

It is further urged that the teaching of human rights in greater depth should be undertaken in universities and similar institutions of higher learning.

As guidelines for such courses, the following topics are suggested:

1. The history of human rights, including the development of humanitarian international law and rules.
2. The protection of the person under the Law of Human Rights at national and international levels.
3. The protection of minorities under national and international law.
4. The elimination of all forms of racial and religious discrimination.
5. The status of the Universal Declaration of Human Rights and of international instruments on human rights as forming part of customary international law.
6. The status of the person under the international Law of Human Rights.
7. The protection of human rights in armed conflicts.
8. The development of national and international institutions for the protection of human rights.
9. The causes that impede the better protection of human rights' (pp.178-9).

Racism, Discrimination and Apartheid

'One of the most flagrant forms of the violation of human rights is racism – discrimination based on caste, race, colour, or religion and apartheid. The denial of these rights prevents justice being realized and has forced men to resort to violence and war.

Racism is reinforced by social, political, and economic structures which help to perpetuate these relationships, even within religions' (p 179).

Protection of Cultures

'It should be recognized that a myth of superior and inferior cultures contributes to injustices and oppressions . . . As religious leaders we affirm that God is creatively at work in every culture . . .

Members of this Conference urge religions to use all their moral weight in bringing about an end to cultural discrimination which deprives the common patrimony of humanity of the cultural riches acquired so slowly and so laboriously' (p. 181)

Religious Liberty

'The right to religious liberty is an essential right of the human person who should be able to respond freely to the call of God's love, and worship his Creator. The right to make a free act of faith is included within the context of the liberty of conscience of the individual.

By virtue of his place in a social context, and of his function as a member of the community, the human person cannot have individual worship only. The need to guarantee to each person the right to manifest his religion or belief in community with others and in public should be recognized everywhere. While the exercise of religious liberty involves many other human rights, of great importance is the right of association, the right to seek, receive, and impart information, and the right to teach religion or belief.

The universal dimension of religion demands that adherents of a religion or belief be allowed to travel freely and to communicate with co-religionists across national frontiers. Moreover, religious liberty includes the right to express implications of religion or belief in social, economic, and political matters, both at the national and international level.

We stress that religious people should not discriminate against, or consider as inferior, those fellowmen who do not share a religious vision of life.

We recommend that the work of the United Nations be attentively and seriously followed with a view to adopting, in adequate form, the draft international convention on the elimination of all forms of religious intolerance and discrimination on ground of religion or belief.'

The Rights of Conscientious Objectors

'We consider that the exercise of conscientious judgment is inherent in the dignity of human beings and that, accordingly, each person should be assured the right, on grounds of conscience or profound conviction, to refuse military service, or any other direct or indirect participation in wars or armed conflicts. This Conference also considers that members of armed forces have the right, and even the duty, to refuse to obey military orders which may involve the commission of criminal offences, or of war crimes, or of crimes against humanity' (p. 183).

Equal Rights for Women

'The idea of peace presupposes that all human beings, men and women, have equal rights. Yet in most of the countries of the world, developed as well as developing, women are underprivileged. This is clearly a grave social injustice, based mainly on male prejudice but partly also on outdated customs. Since such discrimination also prevails in religious organizations, religious bodies should examine their structures and initiate necessary changes' (p. 184).

5.   *Resolutions were also passed on Vietnam, Southern Africa and the Middle East. It was also agreed to set up a new inter-religious world body to be called The World Conference of Religion for Peace.*

THE WORLD CONFERENCE ON RELIGION AND PEACE

II

The Second Assembly
Louvain (Leuven), Belgium
28 August – 3 September 1974

1. The Louvain Declaration
2. Commission I on Disarmament and Security
3. Commission II on Economic Development and Human Liberation
4. Commission III on Human Rights and Fundamental Freedoms
5. Commission IV on Environment and Human Survival
6. Religion and Population
7. Violence and Nonviolence
8. Other Reports

The full proceedings of the Louvain Assembly are published in *World Religion/World Peace*, ed. Homer A. Jack, WCRP, New York 1979.

1. The Louvain Declaration

'I walk on thorns, but firmly, as among flowers.'

The Second World Conference on Religion and Peace, meeting at the University of Leuven/Louvain in the summer of 1974, longs to speak directly to all religious communities of our troubled planet.

Buddhists, Christians, Confucianists, Hindus, Jains, Jews, Muslims, Shintoists, Sikhs, Zoroastrians and still others, we have sought here to listen to the spirit within our varied and venerable religious traditions. Whatever our religion, we know that we are one with the whole of humanity and that all of its problems are our problems. Our faith compels us to search for effective, viable solutions. We have faced together the enormity of the perils presently threatening the human species and its home. We have looked hard at the massive evidence of the political, economic, social and cultural offences against humanity that are inherent in the growing world disorder. We have grappled with the towering issues that our societies must resolve in order to bring about peace, justice and an ennobling quality of life for every person and every people. Drawing upon the inexhaustible resources of our several spiritual heritages, we have experienced together the truth expressed by one of the poets in our midst: 'I walk on thorns, but firmly, as among flowers.'

Our debt to the historic First World Conference on Religion and Peace, held in Kyoto, Japan, in 1970, is very great and gratefully acknowledged. High standards for the ministry of peace and justice in all religions and lands were set forth at Kyoto, and here in Louvain, we have been able to go forward because of their guidance. Of all the things learned at Kyoto, none has marked us more deeply than the discovery that the integrity of the commitment of each to his own religious tradition permits, indeed nurtures, loving respect for the prayer and faithfulness of others. We have contemplated together the inalienable dignity of every human being, as it is affirmed by each of our traditions.

We rejoice that through the profound experiences of conferences like these, and multi-lateral dialogues undertaken by official religious institutions, the long era of prideful, and even prejudiced, isolation of the religions of humanity is, we hope, now gone forever. We are resolved henceforth to serve humanity together each in the way most in keeping with the convictions of his spiritual family and local circumstances.

War Cannot Be Avoided: It Can Only Be Overcome

Peace can no longer be regarded as an ideal which may be cherished or discarded at will. It is a practical and immediate necessity arising out of the present situation where men have acquired such immense power that they are now in a position to conquer the stars or to annihilate themselves completely along with the globe they live on. We therefore dedicate ourselves to work together for the total abolition of war.

We plead with all people of faith and good will to recognize that there is no future for humanity if world-wide nuclear war is simply postponed or temporarily avoided. The delicate 'balance of terror' has given the super-powers, and all other nations with them, nothing more than a reprieve – a little time to concert action to end the nuclear arms race. We urge that the religions of the world mount every possible pressure on the nuclear weapon governments to halt the proliferation of destructive nuclear armament and to roll back all existing nuclear weaponry until the stockpiles of nuclear devices have been safely dismantled and destroyed. We also ask all religious bodies to press other governments now capable of initiating nuclear weapons programmes to renounce any such undertaking.

In the four years since our Kyoto Conference, we confess that we have not known how to mobilize religious people so that they might contribute effectively to the prevention of even limited local or civil wars. Bangladesh, the Middle East, Northern Ireland, the Southern Philippines, Southern Africa, Cyprus and Indochina are among those places where the conflicting forces, including the political decision makers, are largely composed of members of our various religious communities.

With utmost grief we recognize that the Indochina War was not ended by the Paris Peace Agreements of January 1973, and that another hundred thousand Indochinese lives have been lost since that disappointing 'peace' was declared. We understand and respect the Vietnamese Buddhist campaign cry: 'DON'T SHOOT YOUR OWN BROTHER.'

Wherever wars are now going on, we express our deep sorrow over the suffering of all who are involved even as we call upon them and their governments to seek alternative solutions through negotiation, mediation or arbitration, as well as to strive for imperative political, economic, social, cultural and moral change by means more appropriate to their respect for life and their vision of human destiny.

Whatever conscientious religious people decide in respect to the use of violence, we urge religious leaders everywhere to work ceaselessly, in the first instance, for the reduction of the level of violence in all social struggles with the final elimination of violence in favour of peaceful solutions as their firm objective. To respond to violence with violence without first seeking to eliminate its cause is to embark upon the course of unending escalation.

Liberation Plus Development = Peace

Peace is a supreme value for all religions, a state of personal and social existence that, according to all prophets and teachers, is far more than mere absence of conflict. The world without war envisaged by our seers is warless because of its health, its wholeness, its intrinsic justice, its at-one-ness with the universe. Therefore, those who truly seek the peace of the nations should begin with the rigorous spiritual disciplines that bring peace in their own hearts, peace in their families, peace in their cities, and peace with the natural world. Such peace is not possible for men and women unless they learn to master themselves, sublimate their combative energies into productive channels, refuse to accept enslavement in any form, and freely offer themselves in the service of their fellowmen and their eternal Lord.

We have come to see human liberation, economic development and world peace as a dynamic triangular process. People liberating themselves become capable of helping others become free. A truly free people constitutes a productive and cooperative society rather than an exploitative and domineering overlord among their neighbourhood. All the inhabitants of the globe today need to progress toward such basic liberation, such genuine self- development, such a harmonious and peaceful world order. Tyrannical systems, elitist ruling groups and some transnational economic enterprises – whether private or governmental – prevent multitudes of people from participating in the shaping of their own future. We encourage every religion to arouse its people to seek resolutely their own integrated liberation and development, and that of their fellow human beings, near and far. With special insistence we turn to those religious communities that are numerous among the affluent and powerful nations, requesting that they act boldly to end every form of domination among the African, Asian and Latin American peoples whether by their governments or their economic and cultural institutions. We press religious people to condemn profiteering by the affluent world from the weakness of the developing countries, or the racist oppression of the black majority by the wealthy white minority as in Southern Africa, working for such fair policies in economic and technical aid, trade and investment as will help all such peoples pursue their own developmental way. We specifically ask all nations to implement the New International Economic Order advocated by the Sixth Special Session of the U N General Assembly, because it is only through a fundamental restructuring of the world's economic system that a just use and distribution of raw resources, trade and monetary policies can be achieved.

With a high sense of religious responsibility for the balanced growth of the human race, we call upon all religions to work for social, economic and population policies in every nation that promise the fullest respect and opportunity for each child, and the most sensitive care of the environment on which his life and that of posterity depends.

The Rights of Man and the Independence of Religion

The peace we seek is nowhere more endangered than in societies ruled by sheer power unlimited by impartial law. Wherever the Universal Declaration of Human Rights is given but lipservice or openly scorned, conflicts are repressed rather than resolved, making violent struggle likely. The United Nations Charter is in harmony with the highest religious insights when it affirms that the love of peace is incompatible with the violation of basic human rights.

We therefore appeal to religious people in every kind of social order to meditate, to pray and to witness for government policies that will hold inviolate the spirit of man, and guarantee his physical and cultural well-being. Where religious communities are surrounded by grave denials of civil and political rights, or the refusal of social, economic or cultural justice, we declare our solidarity with them as they demand freedom for their peoples.

Fundamental independence from all earthly powers and total dependence on the truth that has called them into being is essential for all religions that would offer a fully authentic ministry to society. We therefore ask all religious bodies to strive for their own freedom from entangling alliances, covert or overt, that could limit their freedom to work for the general freedom of man. Vigilantly maintaining the integrity of their own social organizations, religious communities should freely cooperate with all who sincerely seek to advance the cause of justice, peace and human rights in their own lands and beyond.

In their own internal life, we urge that religious communities encourage all those who bear educational responsibilities to include in the spiritual and moral education of youth an important place for the imperative of peace and the means to attain it.

On the world wide front of the struggle to defend and to enhance the dignity of man, the United Nations and its specialized agencies daily undertake many of the tasks religious seers have long urged upon mankind. As the most extensive network of voluntary associations on the earth, the great religious communities here represented can help the United Nations carry forward its appointed work on behalf of peace on earth and justice among all men.

We call upon the religious communities of the world to press their governments to ratify the covenants and conventions that alone can make the United Nations standards operational in the life of the nations. Through study and action, we urge these communities to concern themselves and their governments with the strengthening of the United Nations.

Humble Enough To Survive

The grave human predicament created by the nuclear threat has recently been aggravated by the acute environmental crisis. The fear of instant annihilation is now mingled with the anguished vision of the gradual extinction of life through the depletion, contamination, suffocation of the planet. The dawning realization that the creation of a right relationship between man and nature is an indispensable part of the struggle for peace and justice has brought a new dimension to the work of our Conference.

The religious insight that there is an essential interdependency of all beings and all things is age-old. Now we are still more aware that there must be not war but profound harmony between the human species and the natural world. We plead with our religious communities to evoke among their peoples a fresh sense of awe before the mystery of existence and a recovery of the value of humble self-restraint in the conduct of personal and social life. Men and women motivated by religion should provide mankind with a shining example of simplicity of life-style, getting along with minimal dependence on material things and deriving their happiness from the quality of their spiritual, aesthetic and cultural pursuits.

But the global challenge of the environmental crisis calls for technical and policy changes on a planetary scale. The issues are at once scientific, economic, political and moral. Not only the natural environment we have inherited but the artificial environment we have created must now be examined from the spiritual perspective. Religious people, leading personal lives in sensitive respect for the rights of nature, must also contribute through their choices as citizens and as workers to the development of a new social vision of environmental ethics. In cooperation with scientists, government planners, industrial managers and all those who inform and form public opinion, religious thinkers should seek to shape and implement a technology for contemporary civilization that will safeguard nature and enhance the general quality of our common life. This great goal will require the full realization of the productive capacity of every person and nation in order to give solid meaning to the social justice we seek for the world's burgeoning population. We appeal to the religious communities of the world to inculcate the attitude of planetary citizenship, the sense of our human solidarity in the just sharing of the food, the energy, and all the material necessities which our generous habitat, unlike any other yet perceived in universal space, will continue faithfully to provide if only it is well loved and respected by mankind.

As each of us turns to prayer and meditation, we seek a conversion of heart to bring about the spirit of sacrifice, humility and self-restraint which will further justice, development, liberation and peace. May the spirit that has blessed us in the Conference at Louvain touch all believers who receive this Declaration in churches, gurdawaras, mosques, pagodas, shrines, synagogues and temples throughout the earth. May our message become their message as they address their peoples. May this call for action be heard and heeded by all those who exercise power in the public affairs of mankind.

2. Commission I on Disarmament and Security (pp. 34–8)

The Commission recognizes the need of religions to make their concern for peace more practical and specific. The dangers of both nuclear and non-nuclear weapons are recognized. The right to intervene in a country's 'internal affairs' when human life is threatened is recognized. It is suggested that smaller nations might hand over their security to the UN and disband their armies. The UN would, therefore, need a permanent army.

Religions should be practical

'The time has come to bring the ideal of peace enshrined in all our religions to the level of practicality. Only in this way will religion be able to influence public opinion and help create a political will towards a more positive peace policy' (p. 34).

Peace and justice cannot be achieved by force

'We reject the whole conception that peace and security can be established, or justice done, by the use of national armed force.' To uphold the rule of law the UN must be given 'the strongest moral support by world opinion' and a permanent UN peace-keeping force should be set up (p. 34).

The strategy of 'mutual assured destruction' is rejected. There is a call for the ending of nuclear weapon tests and for measures to stop the proliferation of nuclear weapons. The call for a world disarmament conference is supported.

It is suggested that small countries could contribute to disarmament by entrusting their security to the UN 'and by giving up their military power' (p. 36).

The horrific effects of non-nuclear weapons is noted, such as napalm and fragmentation bombs. Chemical weapons as well as biological weapons should be banned. The arms trade should be brought under effective control.

Human life is more important than national sovereignty

The international community should intervene where human life is threatened and not regard this as an 'internal' affair. 'We assert that under no circumstances must an internal affair of a nation which involves the destruction of human lives be regarded as an internal or domestic matter in which the UN should not interfere to ensure safety of human lives everywhere. We strongly urge all states to accept the compulsory and binding jurisdiction of the International Court of Justice' (pp. 34–5).

Disarmament could help development

The expenditure on arms diverts resources from development. 'While development must not await disarmament, substantial savings through the reduction of armaments could be diverted to economic and social development' (p. 37).

The Rights of Conscientious Objectors

The right to conscientious objection is again affirmed.

3. Commission II on Economic Development and Human Liberation (pp 39-43)

The report stresses the global emergency. In an interesting use of language, it speaks of human rights in terms of the right to the basic economic conditions for life, rather than in terms of freedom from oppression. 'Liberation' and 'seeking human rights' seem to be used as equivalents, although it is recognized that there is more to the liberation of the human being than meeting basic economic requirements. The report implies that the economic growth of rich countries is at the expense of poor nations. The report ends with a section on the responsibilities of religions, but which is also self-critical of them. There is a call for a World Day of Prayer for Peace, which eventually was to happen at Assisi in 1986.

Economic deprivation is a threat to peace

'As religious leaders dedicated to peace throughout the world, we emphasize that it is the continued deprivation of human rights that constitutes the greatest danger to peace . . . Continuing struggles and conflicts are inevitable unless there is a broader and sharper awareness of social justice at all levels and legislation and social structures adequate to the task of promoting equal opportunity for all. This is a moral issue of the highest order' (pp. 39–40).

Economic policy has a moral dimension

'The experience we have brought to this Conference from our diverse religions and cultural backgrounds unites us in our common purpose to make our message – both critical and creative – heard around the world. We can no longer compartmentalize our moral, economic and social attitudes. It is our moral values and our economic and social behaviour that will determine whether we use technological power to destroy ourselves or to usher in the new era of unprecedented creativity and well-being for everyone which this power makes possible' (p. 40).

Liberation

'Our concern is for human liberation. We believe that in each person the potential is at work to free him or her from self-centredness for a life of freedom and love. Thus a liberated person is one who has the economic basis and political freedom to develop his or her true potential as a human person in keeping with the common good. Each person must be allowed to discover his or her true self and express his or her own authenticity. The liberation of the human being, then, has a deeper dimension than economic; yet without access to food, shelter, education, employment, and health care, there can be no liberation' (p. 40).

The development of the rich is at the expense of the poor

'It has been assumed that the development of the poor countries can take place without any slowing down of the rate of growth of the rich nations. Recent shortages of petroleum and food grains point to the sobering reality that the demands of the rich for scarce resources . . . is severely impairing access by the poor to the supplies' they need . . . It is the 'sinful consumption patterns of the rich societies (not excluding the extravagances of the small number of rich people within the developing countries) that we denounce . . . It is the task of religion to make this criticism and to encourage models of development based on justice' (p. 41).

Religion's task

'It is the special task of religion to stimulate the "conscientization" of the public in order to build a public opinion that leads to political action. In order to be credible, religion must first be critical of itself, willing to examine its own structures, policies, and priorities in order to ascertain if religion is really living what it advocates. There is still, in our view, too much inward concentration of religion which makes it appear more interested in self-preservation than in acting as a catalyst for social change. Often religious groups and institutions have been sidetracked from their real aim to become ideological instruments perpetuating unjust structures. Religion will be credible in the modern world to the extent that it risks its own security in promoting integral human development.

The task of religion is to educate each person to his or her social responsibilities. This sense of human justice must be more adequately reflected in our prayers or meditations. Recognizing our own personal limitations, we emphasize the need for prayer or meditation as a means to foster the spirit of sacrifice, humility, and selflessness which is necessary for justice and peace. To this end, we support a World Day of Prayer and Meditation for Peace. This is an opportunity for all believers and persons of goodwill in their own way earnestly to pray or meditate for the strength and the will to lead in the struggle for economic development and human liberation.

All local religious groups and congregations should devote a specific proportion of their annual budgets to development projects . . . Both as a practical matter and a symbolic witness, individuals and communities should show their solidarity with the deprived by developing a simpler style of life and by changing their own patterns of consumption. Religion must be seen first and foremost as the service of suffering mankind' (pp. 42–43).

4. Commission III on Human Rights and Fundamental Freedoms (pp. 44-51)

This report affirms the points made at Kyoto. It surveys developments in many parts of the world and includes a specific reference to the human rights abuses in the republic of Korea. The need for the UN to find ways of intervening in nation states before genocide occurs is again stressed. Reference is made to the needs of immigrants. Considerable attention is given to the role of religious organizations in upholding human rights and eleven types of action being undertaken by religious bodies in many parts of the world are listed. The ultimate guarantee of human rights is the individual human conscience.

The importance of the individual's conscience

Despite legal steps, 'nothing can possibly be achieved towards bringing about an effective and lasting protection of human rights unless enforcement involves individual human conscience. The struggle to secure fundamental human rights will be won only by changing the conscience of individuals. Human rights will be respected by states and between states when each individual respects the fundamental rights of every other individual within his or her own sphere, in the family, at work, and in the community in which he or she lives' (p. 46).

The role of religious organizations

'It is the task of religious organizations to seek to find solutions based on love, justice and reconciliation' (p. 45).

'We call upon all religious organizations to lend their weight and authority to the campaign to root out this evil' (torture of detainees, which has been called the 'ultimate human degradation') (p. 46).

'Religious organizations can play an important role in helping to obtain fair treatment for migrants and their families' (p. 47).

Religious organizations can play an important part in improving the implementation of those basic human rights which have, in principle, received almost universal acceptance. 'Unfortunately, religious leaders have not always been active in the defence of human rights and fundamental freedoms. In many countries, however, where human rights are widely suppressed, it is above all the religious leaders who have been able to present a challenge to the governments . . . This challenge has been based not on political or partisan beliefs but on deeply held religious faith and moral principles inspired by a profound respect for the dignity of each human being, which, in religious insight, is rooted in man's relationship with the eternal and immortal being' (p. 48).

Amongst the eleven specific types of action being taken, mention is made of the spiritual significance of human rights, dissemination of reliable information and of positive achievements in the protection of human rights.

Freedom for writers

'Since information provides the basis for assuring the effective exercise of human rights, we urge that in all countries writers and publishers be guaranteed the freedom to exercise their profession without fear of persecution' (p. 47).

Migrant Workers

'Many agreements . . . confirm the right of each of the world's religious, ethnic, and linguistic groups to preserve its unique cultural heritage. The right has often been denied in practice. We recommend that all states undertake or intensify action to safeguard the rights of all groups to their cultures, according to existing commitments' (p. 47).

5. Commission IV on Environment and Human Survival (pp. 52–7)

This report on the environment is in many ways prophetic. It recognizes human and global solidarity; it calls for a spiritual revolution and new structures in society to foster equality and social justice. Cooperation of religious people with scientists is called for.

The Responsibility of Religious People

'We realize our common responsibility to work for the resolution of the ecological crisis in the interests of the human community and for the welfare of posterity . . . Any effort to bring about a harmonious relationship between human beings and nature is an endeavour for peace.

As religious people we have a duty to involve ourselves in those programmes which promote the environmental health of our planet. We confess that we have not done enough to stimulate awareness regarding these matters. Indeed there seems to be a general apathy in many religious institutions towards these matters. Adherents of all religions have a responsibility to change this state of affairs . . .

We religious people are concerned with the fulfilment of the whole human person and of all human persons in a global setting. The environmental problem is a human problem. It is related to the quality of life. The organic relationship between human beings and nature can only be restored on the basis of a right understanding of the interdependence of all things – animate and inanimate. This is stressed by the different religious traditions and supported by the findings of modern science. We also recognize that the environment is not only a problem to solve, but also an organic mystery for us to discover and realize . . .

All the blessings of life – including life itself – are gifts. Gratitude on our part is the proper response. Exploiting nature for selfish indulgence and luxuries is an ungrateful sin and a crime against humanity . . . Simplicity of life is to be practised and encouraged . . .

Quality of life does not necessarily mean a higher level of consumption. Rather it refers to an inner transformation of life and civilization for a better coordination between human beings and nature. A spiritual revolution is necessary to bring about this change.

We are bound by a common destiny. We have to take a global view of life and all its dimensions. We are in a space ship, and the available resources are to be shared by all the inhabitants, present and future. Past and present exploitations should be repented. This repentance should take concrete forms of expression.

Natural wealth should be placed under the trusteeship of the world community. Thus we religious people must promote and support those structures and programmes which will foster equality and social justice' (pp. 52–4).

Religion and Science: mutual cooperation

'We see the need for a spiritual dialogue among technicians, scientists, and religious people' (p. 54).

6. Religion and Population (pp. 58–62)

This report begins with a clear statement about the sanctity of human life. It stresses human interdependence. The urgency and complexity of the problems caused by rapid population growth are noted, especially that the greatest population growth occurs in areas of great poverty. Population control and economic development are intertwined. The importance of family life and the need for responsible parenthood are affirmed. There is no specific mention of methods of contraception and the disagreements between and within religions on this subject.

Affirmations

'As religionists from around the world, we make the following affirmations:

We affirm the "given" quality of human life. Life comes to us as a gift and has, in itself, inherent sanctity. Therefore, the human is the criterion in any acceptable solution.

We affirm therefore that world development must be human-centred, assuring equal opportunities for all for fullness of life, human dignity and social and economic justice.

We affirm that each bears responsibility for the other and that, within that mutual responsibility, we are required to strive for liberation, freedom and full humanity for all.

We affirm the value of the family as the centre for nurture, love, compassion, and the development of human potential.

Population level and population growth are world problems calling for the mobilization of world resources – spiritual, ethical, political, cultural and material – towards their equitable solution' (p. 58).

Responsible Parenthood

All our religious traditions place emphasis on the concept of responsible parenthood. Population planning and population policies are not ends in themselves, but a means to a better and fuller life for all. The preservation of the rights of the individual calls in question the right of the state to legislate for compulsory family planning and compulsory birth control measures. There is widespread concern about the family planning programmes being offered to poorer countries in the guise of aid when money is not available for direct developmental programmes. Family planning programmes must not be inconsistent with overall development needs. A prerequisite for all such population control programmes must be full understanding by the participants of the physical, psychological and social effects as well as their voluntary participation.

Responsible parenthood is an obligation. It demands both that there be awareness on the part of parents and that the means be offered by which parents may responsibly determine the size of their family.

Responsible parenthood also demands the recognition of the equality of partners in marriage. Women have rights equal with men in the determination of the size of the family. Full and equal opportunity must be available to women to allow their full human development socially, intellectually, culturally, economically and politically.

Within the context of responsible parenthood, we record appreciation of the strong traditions in various religions of the part played by voluntary restraint in family planning. Such restraint may serve as a model for a more moderate approach to the whole of living' (pp. 60–1).

7. Violence and Nonviolence (pp. 72–3)

This report gives a wide definition of violence. It recognizes that some believers, but not all, are against any use of violence. In violent situations religion should have a reconciling role.

Widespread violence

'Violence is done wherever and whenever the integrity and dignity of the human person are damaged. Thus violence must be seen to be more than physical injury to the person. The unjust and oppressive structures of society itself are violent, inflicting damage upon the human person psychologically as well as economically and socially. The equation of violence with the revolutionary and the radical does not have universal validity; the structures of violence are frequently those of the status quo and conservatism.

The achievement and/or maintenance of economic and political power at the expense of human rights and dignity take many and subtle forms. The prevention of equitable distribution of wealth and resources, the denial of political freedom, the use of torture and psychological means of intimidation –

these are typical examples. The use and perpetuation of such violence usually results in a violent response. Violence breeds violence . . . ' (p. 72).

Violence or Non-violence

'We recognize that the choice of either the violent or nonviolent alternatives in the struggle for freedom and liberation may be made with equal integrity. Some believe that nonviolent action is the only possibility consistent with their religious belief; some are prepared to accept the necessity of violent action as a religious duty in extreme circumstances in the struggle for liberation. One thing is clear, commitment to religious belief, human rights, and the pursuit of social justice for all will not allow us to remain inactive. We must stand on the side of the oppressed' (p. 72).

Victims

'Within the situation of violence both the oppressed and oppressor are victims. Those adopting the nonviolent approach see, as the essential ingredient to their position, love for all those who are victims to the situation, both oppressed and oppressor. They find themselves strengthened by their religious belief in refusing the opposition of violence even in the ultimate organized violence of warfare' (pp. 72–3).

The role of religions

' . . . Religions have a special role of reconciliation. This is a role which needs to be filled not by religious leaders alone, but by the whole body of religious believers. Our own religious structures must come under close scrutiny lest they, too, be part of the violent structures of society. Both the individual followers of the religions and the religious institutions themselves must cultivate sensitive awareness of passive involvement in violence. In addition, since those who exert oppressive violence are frequently members of our religious communities, we have a unique opportunity to confront them with charity' (p. 73).

8. Other Reports

There is further work on a UN Declaration Against Religious Intolerance.

Specific situations are discussed: 'Ending The War in Indochina', 'Southern Africa' and The Middle East, Northern Ireland, Cyprus and Southern Philippines.

THE WORLD CONFERENCE ON RELIGION AND PEACE

III
The Third Assembly
Princeton, New Jersey, USA
29 August – 7 September 1979

1. The Princeton Declaration
2. Commission I: Religion and International Economic Justice
3. Commission II: Religion and International Security
4. Commission III: Religion and Human Dignity, Responsibility and Rights
5. Seminar A: Religion, Education and Commitment
6. Seminar B: Strengthening the Spiritual Dimension
7. Seminar C: Multi-Religious Dialogue and Action in Conflict Situations
8. The Opening Multi-Religious Service

The full proceedings are published in *Religion in the Struggle for World Community*, ed. Homer A. Jack, WCRP, New York 1980.

1. The Princeton Declaration (pp i-vii)

Preamble

The Third Assembly of the World Conference on Religion and Peace (WRCP III), meeting at Princeton in 1979, is the continuation of an important heritage. The first World Conference on Religion and Peace at Kyoto in 1970, and the second in Louvain in 1974, revealed on the international level a basic unity of purpose and goal amid diversities of religious belief, and widened the pathway of inter-religious cooperation for peace. In spite of the scars of religious strife in some parts of the world, we perceive with joy a growing ferment of mutual understanding and respect among the followers of the great religions. We learned in the first two assemblies of WCRP that, while maintaining our commitment to our respective faiths and traditions, we may respect and understand the devotion of others to their faiths and religious practices.

We pledge ourselves to continue to grow in our mutual understanding and our work for peace, justice, and human dignity. The Assembly is aware that we are approaching not only the turn of the century, but also a turning point in human history, with the survival of world civilization at stake. Therefore, we chose as our theme: Religion in the Struggle for World Community.

We rejoice in the sign of world community which this conference represents in gathering 354 participants of Buddhist, Christian, Confucianist, Hindu, Jain, Jewish, Muslim, Shinto, Sikh, Zoroastrian, and other religions from 47 countries around this common theme. We know that forces which negate human dignity are strong and all around us. We see the menace of deadly nuclear weapons and desperate national insecurity. Technological and economic power often exploits and excludes the poor of the world. Political power often represses dissidents and denies human rights. Human greed also destroys the natural environment on which we all depend. We realize that our religious insights and actions were only one contribution to the struggle against these forces. We therefore met with humility but with urgency to face, with the resources of our traditions and beliefs, the danger before us and the world.

Peace Is Possible: Our Conviction

World community, built on love, freedom, justice, and truth, is another name for peace. It is the goal of all our striving. It is not a utopian dream. Despite the temptation to despair as competition for dwindling resources grows more fierce, as centres of economic power intensify their exploitation, and as stockpiles of nuclear weapons grow, we have come together in a spirit of hope. In our various religions, we know that we are members of one human family. Sustained and motivated by the spiritual power by which we all live, we believe that there is an alternative to violence. *We believe that peace is possible.*

This is the hope we would share, not only among ourselves, as followers of our various religions, but with the whole world. We dedicate ourselves to the task of becoming more effective agents of building community. We call upon believers and all human beings to share this hope and to join in a commitment to work for its realization.

We believe that, as religious people, we have a special responsibility for building a peaceful world community and a special contribution to make.

On the one hand, we realize that far too often the names of our various religions have been used in warfare and community strife, and that we must work harder against this. *We cannot deny that:*

the practices of our religious communities are sometimes a divisive force in the world;

too often we conform to the powers of the world, even when they do wrong, rather than confronting those powers with the teachings of our religions;

we have not done enough as servants and advocates of suffering and exploited human beings; and

we have done too little to build interreligious understanding and community among ourselves on the local level where prejudices run strong.

On the other hand, we have been brought to a new awareness, in this assembly, of the deep resources we share for making peace, not only among ourselves, but in the world.

Adhering to different religions, we may differ in our objects of faith and worship. Nevertheless, in the way we practise our faith, we all confess that the God or the truth in which we believe transcends the powers and divisions of this world. We are not masters, but servants and witnesses, always being changed and disciplined in worship, meditation, and practice by the truth which we confess.

We all acknowledge restraint and self-discipline in a community of giving and forgiving love as basic to human life and the form of true blessedness.

We are all commanded by our faiths to seek justice in the world in a community of free and equal persons. In this search, conscience is given to every person as a moral guide to the ways of truth among us all.

We believe that peace in world community is not only possible, but is the way of life for human beings on earth, as we learn it in our prayers or meditation and by our faiths.

These convictions we share. Therefore we can go further and share a common confidence about the fruits of religious witness in the world. *We trust that*:

the power of active love, uniting men and women in the search for righteousness, will liberate the world from all injustice, hatred, and wrong;

common suffering may be the means of making us realize that we are brothers and sisters, called to overcome the sources of that suffering;

modern civilization may someday be changed so that neighbourly good will and helpful partnership may be fostered; and

all religions will increasingly cooperate in creating a responsible world community.

In this confidence, we turn to particular areas where peace and world community are at stake.

Mobilization for Peace: Our Struggle

A. A Just International Economic Order

It is an affront to our conscience that 800 million people in the developing world still live in poverty, that hundreds of millions more are destitute because they are physically unable to work, and that 40 per cent of the world's population cannot read or write. The gap of economic disparity between the developed and the developing countries has widened during the current decade. In view of the stress laid by all the great religions on social and economic justice and the right of all men and women to have a share in the earth's bounty, we call on religious people throughout the world to work for a just and equitable economic order where dignity and humanity in harmony with nature will not be denied to any person.

Such a new international economic order of growing justice and equity would stimulate all nations to achieve viable and self-reliant national economies, capable of participating in international trade on a basis of equality rather than dependence. In order to establish this new vision, there must be the political and social will to promote balanced economic growth worldwide and to allocate its benefits to the abolition of poverty, the meeting of all basic human needs, and the creation of equitable trade relations between the industrial and the developing countries. We call upon religious people to work for the elimination of the structures of economic and social injustice in their respective countries and to mobilize governmental public opinion in favour of anti-poverty programmes. We call on religious institutions with economic resources at their command to work for social amelioration, prevention of destitution, and succour of the poor.

Our sense of religious responsibility impels us to reaffirm that social justice and democratic participation in decision-making are essential to true development. We are of the view that suitable measures should be taken at the national and international levels to ensure that the transnational corporations and enterprises of all economic systems do not wield undue economic, political, and social power in the host country.

All the wealth of the universe is a common heritage held in trusteeship for all. We advocate the rights of yet-to-be-born generations to planetary resources that have been wisely developed rather than wastefully exhausted.

B. Nuclear and Conventional Disarmament

We believe that a major concern for the human family on earth today is the looming danger of nuclear annihilation, either by design or accident. We acknowledge that, in spite of SALT I and II, nuclear arsenals are continuing to grow, imparting a sense of urgency to the need of a world-wide movement to outlaw war and all weapons of mass destruction.

We regard the SALT II treaty between the USA and the USSR as an encouraging development for nuclear disarmament and hope that it will be ratified so that SALT III negotiations may soon begin. It is the duty of organized religion to oppose the proliferation of nuclear weaponry, the arms competition between the USA and the USSR, and the expansion of the conventional arms race throughout the world. Nuclear powers must not use or threaten to use nuclear weapons against nuclear or non-nuclear states.

A global moral and religious campaign which will say NO to ANY KIND OF WAR BETWEEN NATIONS OR PEOPLES is our call to governments, religious groups, and all men and women of conscience and faith. This movement must work towards disarmament and non-violent means of maintaining security. As a prerequisite, it is essential to create an atmosphere of trust and foster a spirit of conciliation between peoples.

In pursuance of these objectives, we propose that the following steps be immediately taken:

a cessation of all testing, research, manufacture, spread, and deployment of nuclear weapons and other instruments of mass destruction;

a comprehensive nuclear test ban treaty;

effective methods of verification to ensure the implementation of these measures; and

a United Nations convention against the use of all weapons of mass destruction, declaring that such use is a crime against humanity.

In order to reduce reliance on arms, we propose that the mechanisms of international security through the United Nations be strengthened, that all nations implement unconditionally all the resolutions of the Security Council, and that the present concept of balance of power be replaced by a system of collective security in accordance with the United Nations Charter.

We express our profound concern over the massive increase in military spending, which has rocketed to $400 billion a year. It seems a cruel irony that, while millions sleep with hungry stomachs, nations and their governments devote a great part of their resources to armaments, ignoring the demands of social justice. We therefore appeal to the members and leaders of our respective communities to use every political and moral influence to urge a substantial reduction in the current military expenditures of their own nations and the utilization of the funds thus saved for development around the world.

C. Human Rights

We reaffirm our commitment, made at Kyoto and Louvain, to the UN Declaration of Human Rights, and we deplore the denial of human rights to any individual or community. We pledge our support to all societies, organizations, and groups sincerely struggling for human rights and opposing their violation. We condemn religious discrimination in any form, and urge the United Nations to adopt a Declaration and Covenant for the Elimination of Intolerance and Discrimination Based on Religion or Belief. We uphold the right of citizens to conscientious objection to military service. We urge religious bodies to press their governments to ratify and enforce all the UN declarations, conventions, and covenants for the protection and promotion of human rights. All the religions to which we owe allegiance enjoin us to protect the weak against the strong, to side with the oppressed against the oppressor, and to respect human life, freedom of conscience and expression, and the dignity of all people. We support the UN declaration and convention against racism and racial discrimination and urge all governments to adhere to them. The actions of the United Nations against apartheid should be implemented by all States, organizations, and individuals.

Noting that WCRP III coincides with the United Nations-sponsored International Year of the Child, we reaffirm our belief in the United Nations General Assembly's 1959 declaration that humanity 'owes the child the best it has to give' and that the child should be brought up 'in a spirit of understanding, tolerance, friendship among peoples, peace, and universal brotherhood'. We appeal to religious people throughout the world to help promote and work for the adoption of social, economic, and population policies in every country so as to assure a better and a brighter future for every child. It is profoundly important that youth be actively involved in the movement of religion for peace, and interreligious gatherings of youth should be encouraged.

We affirm that all human beings are born free and for freedom, that they are equal in dignity and rights, and that any discrimination on grounds of sex is incompatible with human dignity. We are convinced that practices, prejudices, or laws that prevent the full participation of women along with men in the political, social, economic, cultural, and religious life of their countries are morally indefensible and should be eliminated.

D. Environment and Energy Crisis

The earth is threatened increasingly by human misuse of the environment in quest of material prosperity. We are endangering future generations by our depletion of non-renewable natural resources, our pollution of air and water with chemical and radioactive wastes, and our over-exploitation of the soil in many parts of the world. An energy crisis stares us in the face. With diminishing supplies of oil, nations and individuals will have to make sacrifices, develop alternative – if possible renewable – sources of energy, and even change their life-styles. The resources of all religions are needed to cultivate respect for the natural world in which we live, conservation of its resources, and a style of human life that is in harmony with all of nature.*

The children of the earth must conserve our planet's limited resources so that the bounty of the earth may not be wasted.

E. Education for Peace

The world's religious bodies must undertake major educational programmes to increase mutual appreciation of all peoples and cultures, and foster a

* The Assembly took note of the views of some of the participants that there should be no continuation of the development of nuclear power.

commitment to the values of peace. Our efforts so far have not been sufficient. We therefore rededicate ourselves to the education of children, youth, and adults, to the training of our religious leaders, and to the promotion of values of peace and understanding in our conduct in personal and public life.

Ultimately, peace and justice move toward the salvation and wholeness of all humanity, and flow from them as well. We, as followers of great religions, should be the channels through which spiritual power can flow for the healing of the world. We confess that we have not been worthy of this high calling, but we pledge ourselves here anew to be its faithful servants and witnesses. World peace in world community, with justice for all, is possible. We believe that the faith and hope which brought us together in this Assembly have been nurtured and strengthened during our time together. If this faith and hope were to be shared in the same way through the whole life of the religions to which we belong, then, at last, a new force would be brought to bear in human affairs and a new era would begin in the world. We shall pray or meditate, as well as work, that this new era may be realized.

2. Commission I: Religion and International Economic Justice (pp. 106–8)

This report is noteworthy for its careful consideration of what religions can do to promote economic justice. The characteristics of a new and just order are outlined, as a sort of check-list. The economic order puts the person at the centre. It stresses the need for people to be able to participate in decisions which effect their lives.

What can religions do?

'We are in anguish when, looking within ourselves, we recognize the part that we and our religious organizations play in creating, and even perpetuating, the current situation. That situation is not order but chaos which, through structural injustice, brings tragic consequences for hundreds of millions of suffering people. We are compelled by our respective religions to work to rectify that oppression and to seek the material liberation of the poor and the moral liberation of the rich.

'Human dignity is a major theme in the teachings of all religions . . . ' (p. 106). 'Through our religions, we can deepen consciousness of the basic unity of humanity through an individual and national change of heart. We can demonstrate, in our multi-religious, shared life, that world community is actually possible. We can issue timely denunciations of every violation of the fundamental unity of humankind, such as all forms of discrimination: classism, racism, sexism, and any other ideas that divide the human family into hostile camps.

We can teach and witness for ethical standards in economic relations: assisting the powerless in the struggle for empowerment, joining in the drive for economic and cultural decolonization, calling on our governments to curb the abuses of many national and transnational enterprises, accelerating the economic development of the poor, while supporting international agreements which promote more equitable trade relations.

We can study any investments which our various agencies and foundations may hold in the stock of corporate business, investigating how the firms in which agencies are shareholders actually operate at home and abroad in respect of human rights and welfare, urging that they use their leverage as stockholders to press these enterprises to follow principles and practices that promote genuine human development. We can use our other economic assets – land, buildings, and income – to help people attain a better quality of life; for example, through agricultural research and training, and more productive land usage. We can make urban properties serve urban needs, and utilize income in ways that foster self-sufficiency.

We can advocate the rights of yet-to-be-born generations to planetary resources that have been wisely developed rather than wrongfully exhausted.

The universe – its wealth, beauty, and promise – is the common heritage of us all. All religions cherish the universe and strive to live in harmony with it' (p. 108).

A just new order

'The new order which we seek places the person at the centre. No one can be fully human while being the victim of oppressive power ... People's participation is necessary in the achievement of a just, viable, and sustainable order leading to peace' (pp. 106–7).

'World opinion would encourage each society to pursue its own vision of human development' (p. 107).

'Planetary production would be oriented toward the meeting of the basic human needs ... avoiding the stimulation of artificial life-styles and wants, the destructive use of natural resources and unnecessary consumption.'

'Every person would have the right to engage in productive work' (p. 107).

3. Commission II: Religion and International Security (pp. 109–11)

This is a strong statement against weapons of mass destruction. As steps to the elimination of nuclear weapons, there is a call for a ban on all testing and research. Reliance on conventional weapons should be reduced and the United Nations strengthened. Nuclear-weapon states should jointly undertake not to be the first to use such weapons. The threat to peace caused by social injustice is highlighted. The emphasis on non-violence is stronger than at previous conferences.

Social justice is vital for peace

'The most urgent service we can render for peace and security is to insist on social justice and the preservation and restoration of a healthy natural environment, as well as the conservation and recycling of natural resources all over the world. If the injustice which is visited upon millions of people on earth – causing indignities of hunger and destitution – can be lifted, then there can be a better chance to establish security, achieve disarmament, and ban all weapons of mass destruction (atomic, biological, chemical). Similarly, minorities should be treated justly and equitably in order to lessen tensions' (p. 110).

The United Nations and Other International Bodies

'We urge strenuous and concerted efforts aimed at the revision of the United Nations Charter, including the elimination of the veto power in the Security Council and making recommendations of the General Assembly into decisions binding on Member States.

The need exists to strengthen the International Court of Justice, so that offenders who commit crimes against humanity – such as the production, sale, and use of weapons of mass destruction – or crimes against their own people, might be brought to justice.

The establishment of a Court of Moral Authority, to which groups may appeal, might be explored. The religions of the world can help enforce moral authority, at national and international levels, through awareness building within public opinion.'

Religious responsibility

'We call upon religious people in every country to make peace-making an essential part of their religious life' (p. 111).

Non-Violent Action

'We urge all religious people to use non-violence to help assert the human rights of individuals.

We recommend that non-violent actions in the past become a subject in the teaching of history' (p. 111).

'We pledge our support to all individuals protesting the prior claims of disarmament even to the point of civil disobedience' (p. 111).

4. Commission III: Religion and Human Dignity, Responsibility and Rights (pp. 112–17)

After a moving description of the suffering of many people, the report gives a list of the resources of religious institutions which should be used in the struggle for social justice and human dignity. Certain norms of government behaviour which are necessary for the preservation of human freedom and dignity are outlined. Specific attention is paid to South Africa, to Racial and Ethnic Discrimination, in particular the plight of 'so-called untouchables' and of the Greek ethnic community in Istanbul, to Refugees, to Religious Minorities, to the Unborn, to the Child, to Youth, to Women and to the Elderly.

Religious resources available to be used in the struggle for social justice and human dignity

'We believe that our action on behalf of social justice is in itself a religious activity. Thus in taking stock of the resources inherent in religious institutions and in their leaders, we discovered that at least the following resources can and should be directed toward the struggle for social justice and human dignity:

Our significant potential for influencing political and legislative people and events.

Our moral/ethical insights which can be used in evaluating public policy. What is legal is not necessarily moral.

Our knowledge of both the norms and the true essence of our religions. These can help us expose and oppose situations in which our religions are used to give authority to practices which are contradictory to the fundamental tenets of our faith.

Our access to the grass roots level where we enjoy high credibility. This gives us an information network which can be used for the cause of human dignity.

Our doctrines which stimulate clarity and compassion. Because we believe in human values and equality on a religious level, we have an even deeper motivation and justification for working for human dignity.

Our spiritual resources such as prayer, meditation, solidarity, discipline and forebearance, self-criticism and introspection.

Our position, often as a religious majority. Here we have a special responsibility to speak out for freedom of religion and equality of treatment for people of minority religions' (p. 113).

The Politically Oppressed

'We agreed that, for the preservation of human freedom and dignity, human governance must recognize and institute the following necessary conditions:

1. Respect for the value of individual life.

2. A standard of living in consonance with basic human needs.
3. Freedom to participate in the decision-making process of government.
4. A political, social and economic structure which is just for all.
5. Living conditions free from violence.
6. Procedures and mechanisms for redress when human rights are violated'
   (pp. 113–4).

The Unborn

'We believe that human life is sacred . . . Although we could not come to a common understanding of the serious moral issues involved in the question of abortion, nevertheless we agree that the question of abortion only illustrates a symptom' (pp. 116–7).

5. Seminar A: Religion, Education and Commitment (pp. 118–22)

This report stresses the important role that religious communities can play in education for peace. It points to the need for peace education in Religious Training Institutions, within Religious Groups, in Other Communities and through the Mass Media. The suggestions for the training of religious leaders are interesting, although seldom yet adopted.

Religion's role in peace-education

'The world's religious bodies must undertake major educational programmes to increase awareness of peace issues, appreciation of all peoples and cultures, and commitments to the value of peace. Education is one of our greatest resources. At its best, it is a non-violent form of power; it builds community by increasing understanding; it enriches the whole person. And it is an activity in which our religious bodies have considerable competence and experience' (p. 118).

Education for Peace in Religious Training Institutions

'Course content in institutions training religious leadership should include subjects such as social justice, other religions, the causes of racism and injustice, non-violent resolution of conflict . . . '
　'It should be impressed on future religious leaders that the sharing of one's faith is to be considered more an offering of a precious gift than an indiscriminate proselytizing.'
　'In addition to the training of students, religious leaders have a responsibility to use their moral authority to speak truth to power, e.g. to governments. In this

regard, a combined statement of various faiths carries more weight than a statement from only one faith.'

'Teaching about a religion should, if possible, be done by a person of that faith' (p. 119).

6. Seminar B: Strengthening the Spiritual Dimensions (pp. 123–8)

The report recognizes that this was the first time at a WCRP Assembly that a group had addressed common spiritual foundations in the formation of world community. A number of specific suggestions were made for strengthening the spiritual basis of peace-building and the work of WCRP. Interfaith meditation is commended. The failure of religions to be channels of peace is recognized, but the group believed that peace is possible when empowered by spirituality.

Interfaith Meditation

'Collective interfaith meditation among persons of different traditions promotes the unity of the human family. For the promotion of peace among communities, all efforts must be made to expand collective meditation in different localities. This is relevant to the work of WCRP. Congregational prayer brings the group close to the divine and also persons in a group close to each other. Interfaith congregational prayers will bring together persons of different traditions. Repeated congregational meditation and chanting also promotes togetherness' (p. 125).

7. Seminar C: Multi-Religious Dialogue and Action in Conflict Situations (pp. 129–35)

This report includes discussion of a number of specific situations and suggests concrete action that could be undertaken by WCRP. It ends with a summary of views that could be endorsed by most members of all religions.

Agreements

'Although there may be differences of opinion, both within a particular religious community and between different religious communities, on the analysis of conflicts and the nature of the remedies suggested, there are certain points which may be endorsed and proclaimed loudly by all religious people:

1. A total rejection of all forms of violence which offend human dignity: namely, torture of all forms; indiscriminate killing of innocent men, women and children; holding innocent persons as hostages; and the oppression of one class or caste in society . . .
2. Looking after or helping families of those who are imprisoned or killed in the struggle for justice should be regarded as a religious duty, not just as a charity.
3. Religions can exercise a critical function in situations of conflict . . . Religions should not allow themselves to be used by political powers or parties . . .
4. Non-violent action to resolve conflicts has not received the serious attention it deserves in recent years . . .' (p. 134).

8. The Opening Multi-Religious Service (pp. 144–5)

The opening service included a litany in which all were invited to join and an Affirmation of Our Need for Repentance. The Litany has a strong sense of shared values.

Remembering Our Work Together: WCRP I, Kyoto Declaration 1970
Reader: Dr Homer A. Jack

Reader: As we sat down together facing the overriding issues of peace we discovered that the things which unite us are more important than the things which divide us.
We found that we share:
All: A conviction of the fundamental unity of the human family, and the equality and dignity of all human beings;

Reader: We found that we share:
All: A sense of the sacredness of the individual person and his conscience;

Reader: We found that we share:
All: A sense of the value of the human community;

Reader: We found that we share:
All: A realization that might is not right; that human power is not self sufficient and absolute;

Reader: We found that we share:
All: A belief that love, compassion, selflessness, and the force of inner truthfulness and of the spirit have ultimately greater power than hate, enmity, and self interest;

Reader: We found that we share:

All: A sense of obligation to stand on the side of the poor and the oppressed as against the rich and the oppressors;

Reader: We found that we share:
All: A profound hope that good will finally prevail.

Reader: Because of these convictions that we hold in common, we believe that a special charge has been given to all men and women of religion to be concerned with all their hearts and minds with peace and peace-making, to be the servants of peace.

Affirmation of our need for repentance

All: As men and women of religion, we confess in humility and penitence that we have often betrayed our religious ideals and our commitment to peace. It is not religion that has failed the cause of peace, but religious people. This betrayal of religion can and must be corrected. We pledge ourselves to try to do so.

WORLD CONFERENCE ON RELIGION AND PEACE

IV

The Fourth Assembly

Nairobi, Kenya

23–31 August 1984

1. The Nairobi Declaration
2. Commission I: People of Faith Working Together for Peace
3. Commission II: Human Dignity. Social Justice and Development of the Whole Person
4. Commission III: World Peace and Disarmament
5. Reports of Working Groups

The full proceedings are published in *Religions for Human Dignity and World Peace*, ed. John B. Taylor and G. Gebhardt, WCRP, Geneva 1986

1. The Nairobi Declaration * (pp. i-vi)

In Nairobi in 1984, we of the World Conference on Religion and Peace have met in our Fourth World Assembly. We have come, nearly 600 of us, from 60 countries and from most of the world's religious traditions – Buddhist, Christian, Confucian, Hindu, Jain, Jewish, Muslim, Shinto, Sikh, Zoroastrian, the traditional cultures of Africa and North America, and others. From our diversity of cultures and traditions, we have come to address a theme of urgent common concern: Religions for Human Dignity and World Peace. We address these goals of human dignity and world peace together, for they are inextricably linked and must be pursued together.

Our previous Assemblies in Kyoto in 1970, Louvain in 1974, and Princeton in 1979 have been milestones in the growth and work of WCRP as we strive for peace, united by a spirit of co-operation. In Nairobi, in 1984, we find ourselves at a major turning point.

* Adopted by general agreement and without dissent at the closing session.

In the five years since we last met, the world has seen little progress in either the cherishing of human dignity or the movement toward world peace. While the nuclear arms race has continued to escalate in its staggering expenditures, in its rhetoric, and its incalculable danger, the massive human needs of poverty, hunger, unemployment, and lack of education have been grossly neglected. Militarization of societies, trade in arms, recourse to violence, religious and ideological intolerance, and assaults on human rights continue. The structures of economic and political oppression which perpetuate the privilege of a few at the expense of the masses are still firmly in place.

We are encouraged, however, by the widening awareness and public consciousness of the dangers and costs of our present world situation and by the world-wide growth of grass-roots movements expressing the determination of people everywhere for change. It is time for new strategies and priorities for peacemaking, and for renewed commitment to our work.

We have met in Nairobi as men and women rooted in our religious traditions, and linked to one another in vision and action. We acknowledge the painful fact that religion too often has been misused in areas of strife and conflict to intensify division and polarization. Religious people have too often failed to take the lead in speaking to the most important ethical and moral issues of our day and, more importantly, in taking steps toward change. In meeting together, we have not turned from self-criticism or from very difficult discussions of sensitive issues. And yet our affirmation is one of hope.

The Nairobi Assembly has changed us. The new participation of over one hundred youth delegates has given us the vitality and vision of a new generation, eager to join hands in concrete interreligious projects for peace. The strong and energetic contribution of over 150 women made clear the necessity of women's equal partnership, not only in family life, but in the leadership of religious communities and social and political institutions. Over half of us are participants from Asia, Africa, and Latin America, who have called WCRP to a deeper understanding of our global interrelatedness in working for peace.

Through our struggle, we have been able to build trust. We have shared in worship and meditation. We have discovered once again that our differences of culture and religion, far from being a threat to one another, are a treasure. Our multiplicity is a source of strength. We bear the testimony of experience that world community is possible. From our diversity of traditions, we are united in faith and hope, and in our common pursuit of human dignity and world peace.

I. The Context of Africa

Africa has not only been the place of this Assembly; Africa and the concerns of its peoples have shaped the very context and perspective of our discussions. The African traditional cultures have a strong spirit of community and family, and a vibrant sense of the wholeness of life. Many religious traditions now live together in the continent of Africa – the traditional religions, along with

Christianity, Islam, Hinduism, Jainism, Sikhism and Judaism. The many religious communities of Nairobi have welcomed us and given us a sense of the riches and challenges of living together in the pluralistic society of Kenya.

The peoples of Africa have also experienced sharply the very issues we have addressed in our Assembly and have helped us all to see these issues more clearly. The affront to human dignity of the apartheid regime in South Africa calls us to repudiate separation and division and to seek the community of all races. The cry of human needs in drought and famine, the growing militarism of African governments, the increasing arms trade in Africa, the instances of political intolerance, the penetration of East-West rivalry into African political affairs – all call us to a wide understanding of the dynamics of global insecurity and the effect of global, political and economic structures on the emerging African States.

The new WCRP/Africa is beginning to articulate the common values religious people bring to the creation of a just society. It stresses the need for active engagement in struggles for change and is committed to the realization of a new Africa.

II. Reconciliation in Regional Conflict

We are convinced that a major new priority of WCRP must be to address ourselves to areas of chronic regional tension and conflict – in Southern Africa, the Middle East, South and Southeast Asia, Central America and Europe. Since World War II, over 150 wars, most of them in the Third World, have claimed at least ten million lives. Regional conflicts become swiftly polarized by East and West, and raise the level of instability and insecurity in the entire world.

The roots of these conflicts vary and are complex. But wherever such conflict takes on the language and symbolism of our religious traditions, pitting one against the other, it must be the business of WCRP to be involved, both regionally and with WCRP/International support.

We commit ourselves, as religious men and women, to undertaking the work of reconciliation and peacemaking. We must deal with the issues of religious discord where they arise. We must deal with the economic and political struggles which take on religious rhetoric for narrow or chauvinistic purposes. We must take action, as a multi-religious body committed to peace, in the very areas where religion and peace seem to be in opposition.

III. Disarmament

Disarmament has long been a priority for the work of WCRP, and the urgent necessity of working for disarmament today is undiminished. With one voice, from our various traditions of faith, we insist that nuclear weapons and all weapons of mass and indiscriminate destruction are immoral and criminal, and that the stockpiling of such weapons, with intent or threat to use them erodes the very foundation of moral civilization.

We join the scientists, physicians, educators, and statesmen who have taken an active role in opposing the arms race. We pledge our determined commitment to disarmament as we continue to work as a non-governmental organization at the United Nations, and as we work to influence our religious communities and our nations.

Specifically, we call for an immediate freeze on all further nuclear weapons research, production, and deployment; the strengthening of the Nuclear Non-Proliferation Treaty; a Comprehensive Test-Ban Treaty; and a No First Use commitment on the part of nuclear nations as essential initial steps toward the dismantling of all nuclear arsenals.

Conventional weapons are also instruments of death and oppression. Halting the spread of militarization and the commercial exploitation of developing countries by trade in arms leading to military and political dependency is a crucial part of our commitment to disarmament.

It is a sign of hope for the future that the youth of this Assembly have called for the establishment of ministries and departments of peace to work for the global security that ministries and departments of defence have been unable to realize.

IV. Development

Delegates from Asia, Africa, and Latin America have given us all a new perspective on the arms race, as seen through the eyes of the poor. For the poor, survival is not primarily a question of the future in a nuclear world, but an urgent question of the present in a world beset with hunger, drought, and disease. Our common commitment to peace is based upon the clear interrelatedness between disarmament and development.

Disarmament means liberation, not only from arsenals of weapons ready for use, but from the perpetual fear and insecurity which have accompanied our obsession with the instruments of death. Development means liberation from hunger and poverty; it means a just sharing of the natural and economic resources of the world, and the investment of our energies in life, and in the future.

As men and women of religion, we cannot tolerate the priorities of a world in which there are at least three tons of explosives, but not enough food, for every man, woman and child on earth. We pledge ourselves, through our religious communities and our governments, and through continued WCRP cooperation with the UN, radically to reverse these priorities.

We have a vision of a world in which the economic and political structures which perpetuate injustice and poverty are completely changed, and in which the armaments necessary to maintain these structures of injustice and oppression may be turned to ploughshares for the work of peace.

V. Human Rights

Along with disarmament and development, human rights are an essential part of the total and holistic peace we seek. We mean not only civil and political rights, but the right to live with all the basic economic, social, and cultural rights of a life of fullness and freedom, including religious freedom. We reaffirm our commitment to the UN Universal Declaration on Human Rights, and we insist that these rights are the very basis and foundation of a just and humane society and can never be postponed or suspended in the name of national security.

Our support for human rights must be consistent. Wherever human rights are trampled upon, we must speak out and act. We must resist and unmask the selective and tactical use of human rights issues by nations, especially the USA and the USSR, which raise their voices in one instance and ignore violations in another, as suits their political ends.

Our South African delegates – Hindu, Muslim, and Christian – have all made us sharply aware of the suffering and incalculable violence done to individuals, families, and whole peoples by the racist ideology and 'theology' of apartheid. We commit ourselves to work toward changing the international political and economic structures which support the South African regime.

In our concern for human rights, we must also work regionally and internationally on many other affronts to human dignity. Despite efforts being made by political leaders and religious people, there is deep-seated prejudice resulting in many forms of discrimination against scheduled castes and economically oppressed and socially stigmatized classes in South Asia, against the Burakumin of Japan, and against the indigenous peoples of the Americas, Australia, the Philippines, and elsewhere. The world has many millions of refugees with no right to the roots of home, four million of them in Africa alone. And there are countless human beings stripped of their human rights behind closed doors. They have disappeared; they have been imprisoned without trial; they have been victims of torture. Wherever, and in whatever way, human rights violations occur, it is our concern, internationally and interreligiously.

We support with conviction and hope the 1981 UN Declaration on the Elimination of All Forms of Intolerance and of Discrimination Based on Religion or Belief, and we pledge to support its implementation.

VI. Peace Education

Education for peace is more urgent than ever before. As religious men and women, we pledge ourselves to stressing and raising to public consciousness the foundations of peacemaking within our own religious traditions, through education in temples, churches, mosques, synagogues, and homes. This will require our commitment to planning, training, and funding for peace education programmes. As religious people of action, we must deliberately link our personal lives and daily choices to our wider work as peace-makers.

In our religious institutions, and in schools, colleges and universities, we will encourage new initiatives for peace education. Our public and community life must include knowledge and discussion of the realities of the arms race, the conflicts that lead to war, the means and strategies for non-violent resolution of conflict, and the work of the UN and UNESCO.

Essential to peace education is learning about and coming to understand those of different religions, ideologies, and cultures with whom we share our communities, our nations, and our world. In many cases, the opposite of conflict and violence is knowledge, and so educational efforts must be made that fear may begin to give way to trust. We must strengthen and deepen mutual understanding by sustained dialogue, and by undertaking common work together. We need to understand one another. We need one another in order to see and understand ourselves more clearly. And we need one another in order to undertake together work that will require the resources and energies of people throughout the world.

The spiritual resources of our religious traditions give us strength to dedicate ourselves to the task ahead. We are compelled to turn the faith and hope that sustain us into dynamic action for human dignity and world peace.

2. Commission I: People of Faith Working Together for Peace (pp. 201-6)

Considerable attention was paid to how people of different religions can work together. Different approaches to dialogue were recognized and also the difficulties of dialogue. It was again recognized that 'religion has been a source of conflict in the world' (p. 201). Some practical suggestions were made.

What binds us together

'We have become aware of much that binds us together. Ultimate Reality is infinite, while our ways of describing and understanding it are necessarily finite, so we have learned that we must listen with respect and humility while others worship or describe their spiritual experience. We have also discovered that all of our religious traditions urge compassion and kindness upon their followers, even though we have often failed to live up to our own high calling.

We cannot wait until all outstanding differences are settled before turning to such questions as war, poverty, racism, injustice and oppression. There is a two-fold pattern to our relationships which one of our speakers expressed by saying, "Sometimes we talk face to face, sometimes we talk together to others"' (p. 202).

Approaches to Dialogue

'During our discussion four main approaches to dialogue seemed to emerge, although it is not suggested that this is a comprehensive list. Some called on us to rise above our separate traditions and recognize that the ultimate goal of all religions is the same. They propose that we work for a federation of religions and present a common position in the interests of peace.

Others preferred to think of dialogue as a bridge by which we reach out to others, but which must be firmly anchored at each end. We must be deeply rooted in our own tradition and find within it the dynamic toward peace. Only in this way can we maintain our credibility with others of our own persuasion and engage them also in the search for peace. This is also a reminder that religion cannot be simply boiled down to a set of beliefs but is a closely knit fabric of cultural and personal loyalties, involving an integrated approach to life. At the same time, however, we turn with love and humility to others recognizing that they may have treasures to share with us.

There were those who challenged us to concentrate on common projects and struggle for social justice in the cause of peace, and to discuss theological issues only in so far as they arise within and may in turn support such collaborative effort.

Another set of voices called on us to find our underlying unity in silence. In this spirit monks, nuns and others have come together across religious lines to share in common work and meditation. Indeed, during this Conference some very meaningful moments have occurred when we sat together reflecting quietly.

What can be separated logically on paper cannot be so readily separated in practice. None of these approaches is necessarily exclusive of the other, but it is helpful when engaging in inter-religious dialogue and co-operation to be aware of the sometimes different premises from which we begin' (pp. 202–3).

The Difficulties

'Co-operation between people of different faiths is not simple. We experience, even before we start, barriers of race, gender, language and culture. We come from different backgrounds and different life-situations, as well as from different social, economic and political systems . . . ' (p. 203).

'Historical relationships between our various religions have not always been happy; they have been marred by oppression, persecution and bloodshed. While we cannot undo history we can offer our repentance and make past experiences the basis for a better future' (p. 203).

The group recognized that religious conflicts are still occurring. Religious leaders should declare that these have no religious sanction and that people of different faiths can live together. 'Such declarations will not by themselves stop conflict or eliminate persecution. They will, however, remove from these situations any moral or religious sanction . . . There are also times when religious leaders have a responsibility to take immediate steps and intervene in conflicts, whether local, national or international, which are rooted in religious differences' (p. 203).

The group was already warning of the upsurge of triumphalist and intolerant religious zeal. 'Often their religious convictions have been linked with nationalistic sentiments. While we differ with those who claim that theirs is the only way to truth, we wish to be consistent with our own call to openness and dialogue' (p. 203).

The group recognized the need to work with those of no faith who struggle for peace and justice.

Practical Suggestions

'The world is only now becoming re-acquainted with the ancient spiritual wisdom of people from indigenous religious traditions – whether in Africa, the Americas, the Pacific or elsewhere. These traditions contain many insights, for instance regarding the human relationship to the environment, that we ignore to our great detriment' (p. 204).

'Our schools need to cultivate the love of peace and the abhorrence of war. Textbooks should be examined for militarism, racism, and any form of prejudice' (p. 204).

3. Commission II: Human Dignity, Social Justice and Development of the Whole Person (pp. 207–12)

This report summarizes the presentations of the Consultant-experts, who gave evidence of discrimination in various parts of the world. Some practical suggestions are made, but other than in the opening paragraph, there is no agreed affirmation.

Each Human Being is a Unique Creation

'Each human being is, by his or her very being, a unique creation in this universe, and deserves to be treated with equal dignity, regardless of colour, race, religion, nationality or sex. This is a basic requirement in dealing with human beings in whatever capacity. But this dignity can be maintained only if equal socio-economic and political justice are available to all human beings. Social peace can be maintained only if there is justice as its foundation. The third requirement is equal opportunity to human beings for the full development of the potentialities inherent in each individual' (p. 207).

4. Commission III: World Peace and Disarmament (pp. 213–23)

This report begins with a description of the Commission's work. There are three main sections on Educating for Peace, on Disarmament and on the Middle East.

The first stresses the importance of education for peace, but most of the suggestions had already been made at previous assemblies. The second part, besides some general principles, deals with several specific issues. Predictably the commission was in favour of a comprehensive Test-Ban treaty and the strengthening of the Nuclear Non-Proliferation Treaty. There was strong support for a nuclear freeze and for the prevention of the arms race spreading to outer space. In the section on the Middle East, the commission tried to address a particular flash-point in which religion was one of the significant causes of conflict. Three women from the Middle East, one Muslim, one Jewish and one Christian, agreed a statement which was presented to the Commission. 'All three affirmed the universal humanity of all and the hope that the Divine in each person would be moved by the evidence that religious values can assert themselves under conditions of war' (p. 205). In subsequent discussions, there was a tendency, partly from those who had joined the group at a later stage, to level charges and to seek to pinpoint blame. This shows the great difficulty of religious people reaching any agreement on particular situations of conflict.

Principles of Work for Peace

These include:
'(a) The need for spiritual practices to facilitate a disarming love, even of "enemies". This is part of a holistic approach to disarmament.

(b) The need for us to work within our religions so that the beauty of holiness rather than sectarian suspicion defines our interactions – especially as regards conflict resolution' (p. 215).

The Middle East

From the statement of the three women:
'1. We pledge to honour and respect every race, religion, culture and individual.
2. We recognize the right of each individual to his or her human rights, as described in the UN Charter.
3. We recognize the sovereignty of all countries of the area, including the Jewish state of Israel.
4. We recognize the right of the Palestinian people to self-determination and their right to establish an independent Palestinian state in the West Bank and Gaza Strip' (p. 224).

5. Reports of Working Groups

A(i). How to Dismantle Ethnic and Religious Prejudices Which Act as Obstacles to Building and Sharing Society (pp. 231-3)

This suggests that much prejudice arises from inner conflict, but that true religion promotes inner harmony. The group suggested the pattern of relationships between religions that it would like to see emerge.

'It is only the religious dimension in people's understanding of their own selves and their relation to others, to the universe, and to their creator, that can harmonize these conflicts at the very root of their being. Although religion in itself is perfect, the masses who struggle to reach that perfection are themselves imperfect persons, and it is not strange to see religion itself being employed to promote self-interests of groups and individuals. It is then that religion becomes a casualty. The group, while admitting the existence of all types of discrimination in social behaviour, conceded that if it were resolved at the religious level, it should cover other areas of prejudice such as ethnicity.

If more people are grounded in the true understanding of religion, the more they will see beyond, the easier for them to transcend racial, tribal and all other distinctions that divide man from man.

The group expressed the need for concerted action to present the image of religion as something that extols justice, love and peace, and the concept of religious concern with humanity as something that has no boundaries.

In this regard mention was made of the ways in which religion is propagated and observed by institutions themselves tending to be instruments of discrimination.

It should be clarified that WCRP is not attempting to fashion all religions to achieve some kind of uniformity, but WCRP would be happy if it could contribute toward unity among the adherents of different faiths.

Differences based on traditions, cultures, practices, interpretations, rites and rituals are to be appreciated and respected, but fighting based on misunderstandings, misinterpretations of doctrine and the selfish abuse of religion should be eliminated' (p. 232).

Education

'The working group, while recognizing the difficulties involved in teaching all religions to children at school, recommends that WCRP adopt a policy of encouraging the teaching of the common values contained in all religions, through publication of curricular materials' (p. 233).

A(ii). How to Combat Racial Discrimination As It Survives in Many Parts of the World But is Still Legally Imposed by the Apartheid System in South Africa (pp. 234–8)

This report brands as blasphemy the view that apartheid is the will of God. Here a specific issue, the condemnation of apartheid, gains universal agreement.

'Apartheid, a crime against conscience, brings about hunger, poverty, sickness, imprisonment, suffering, death . . . indeed an endless list of sufferings to the people of South Africa. We, as religious people from many parts of the world, have to make a concerted effort to rid the world of this evil system that violates the fundamental human rights of the majority of the people of South Africa. No religion can remain aloof from the call to end this blasphemy, to put an end to relocation, to homeland rule, and indeed, to the systematic violence in South Africa' (p. 25).

B. How to Overcome Competing, Destabilizing and Proselytizing Religions and Ideologies Which Act as Forces of Disunity and as Threats to Peace in Africa and in Other Parts of the World (pp. 239–41)

This report grapples with the conversionist activities of some religions.

'Although we admit that people of religion have often failed in their relations with people of other faiths, we believe that all religions have within them the spiritual and theological resources that would enable them to contribute to the reconciliation needed between religions and in society as a whole' (p. 239).

Resolution I (p. 240)

'Recognizing that some members of religious traditions so understand their uniqueness that they desire to win converts,

Noting that these beliefs, if presented in a legitimate way (without aggression, coercion or misuse of economic resources or social services), need not prevent a creative co-existence nor a positive cooperation in religious dialogue or social action,

Believing that the correct behaviour of any group often depends on its sense of identity and security, We recommend:
1. That the predominant religion in any situation
    (a) assure the minority religions of respect and full protection;
    (b) refrain from attempts to undermine a minority religion in any way;
    (c) guarantee equal rights and opportunities to the followers of such minorities; and
    (d) not merely tolerate minorities, but accept them as having an authentic position within the religious search for truth.
2. That the minority religion in any situation accept a recriprocal responsibility to respect the traditions and beliefs of the predominant religion, and therefore refrain from becoming a destabilizing influence.

C. How to Spread Education for Peace and Multi-Religious Understanding

Group C gave a wide-ranging definition of religious education for peace.

'Religious education and education for peace are essentially interrelated. Religious education for peace encourages a dynamic process and an all-embracing (holistic) vision: internal and external aspects, private and collective practice, individual and group participation, the respectful preservation of life for generations to come, spiritual fulfilment and a just and harmonious world order. Thus there is the necessity to rethink education for peace within the framework of each religion, according to the realities, and at a multi-religious level' (p. 243).

4. This group drew attention to the influence of women in cultivating peaceful attitudes.

WORLD CONFERENCE ON RELIGION AND PEACE

V

The Fifth Assembly
Melbourne, Australia
January 1989

1. The Melbourne Declaration
2. Commission I: Building Trust Through Disarmament and Conflict Resolution Structures
3. Commission II: Building Trust Through Human Rights and Responsibility in the Family and Global Community
4. Commission III: Building Trust Through Economic and Social Development and Ecological Balance
5. Commission IV: Building Trust Through Non-Violence and Education for Peace.

The above documents are all to be found in *Melbourne Declaration and Reports*, WCRP, Geneva 1990.

1.   The Melbourne Declaration (pp. 1–4)

The Fifth Assembly of the World Conference on Religion and Peace has met in Melbourne, Australia. It records its gratitude that it met in a nuclear weapons free zone. We came, nearly 600 of us, from many of the world's religious traditions and from some 60 countries. A women's meeting and a youth meeting preceded the main conference. 35% of the participants were women, 15% youth. Though we are of different religions, we have all come with a common commitment to seek peace, pursue justice and preserve the sacredness of nature.

We share many feelings. First we feel a sense of hope, stimulated because of developments in the international arena occurring since 1987. The Central American Peace Process brought progress toward the resolution of the tragic conflicts in that region of the world. Fighting has ended between Iran and Iraq, and hope for a speedy conclusion of fighting in Afghanistan follows the planned withdrawal of Soviet troops from that country. Progress has been made toward the withdrawal of South Africa from Namibia and the complete independence of that country. In the field of disarmament, the Intermediate-range Nuclear Forces Treaty, concluded by the United States and the Soviet Union, will lead to the dismantling of certain classes of nuclear weapons. The recent world conference in Paris condemning the use of poisonous gas in warfare may indeed lead to the end of the production, stockpiling and use of chemical weapons.

Many people have shared the hope in the potential end of the cold war. Freedom and democracy have become realistic goals in countries long noted for their dictatorial systems. In some nations where the concept of the national security state has resulted in internally repressive regimes, democratic practices are once again emerging with the prospects of renewed rights and freedom. Changes in the Middle East increase the potential and the necessity for the Israeli-Palestinian conflict to be resolved. The agreement reached at the Vienna Conference [CSCE] raises new hopes for human rights in Europe. The world-wide ecological crisis is creating a new awareness of our global interdependence and the necessity to find ways of preserving the environment.

The conception of the sacredness of the land and our unity with it is deeply felt in many places in the world. In many countries people of differing cultures and religions are striving to find ways of creating pluralistic societies. And around the world religious people are meditating and praying together for peace as in Assisi, 1986; Mt Hiei, 1987; and elsewhere.

Second, we share a sense of anticipation as the twentieth century draws to a close. We hope to enter the next century with a better understanding of our common humanity and common destiny. The conflicts and problems of the twentieth century should not be allowed to enter or destroy the twenty-first century. Signs of hope exist. In Europe a political-economic community will come into being in 1992, committed to unity within and peaceful relations without. Hong Kong and Macao will be reunited with the People's Republic of China by the end of the century, ending an era of colonial rule. There is growing consciousness of the need to resolve the global debt crisis and create a more just and sustainable economy. This is accompanied by critical self-examination by many national governments of their economic, social, political and cultural policies. Words such as freedom identity, minority rights, openness and reconstruction now have new meaning. A vision of a world community is beginning to take shape.

Third, there is an increased awareness of the importance of moral values in human life. Humanity can shape matters of life and death. We need not be subject to blind fate or political forces beyond our reach. Rationality and technology are not the ultimate values of human existence. Human rights are not to be defined by or for political and other conveniences but defended because of their inherent values.

Fourth, the United Nations is being revitalized, as nations have once again begun to use the UN as an effective instrument for achieving and sustaining peace, justice and freedom. We rejoice that the United Nations peace-keeping force has been awarded the 1988 Nobel Peace Prize. The special effort of the UN to conclude a Convention on the Rights of the Child, has focused concern upon the world's children, those who will inherit the situation we have created for the twenty-first century.

Fifth, educational systems involving the media and other forms of communication are being developed in order to educate people for peace and justice, creating respect for all peoples, cultures and faiths.

Finally, a willingness on the part of many religions is emerging whereby they contribute their finest and deepest inspirations and co-operate with each other and with all who share common concerns in order to achieve lasting peace, a humane social and physical environment, a world not suffering from poverty, oppression, often avoidable sickness and death, including the ravages of AIDS, endemic wars, discrimination and the other powers that plague our peoples.

We are grateful for these signs of hope, because five years ago the Nairobi Assembly met in a context of despair. Yet we are also realists. The nuclear threat still exists. Chemical weapons have been used in recent years. Many countries face incredible debts and remain in conflict with external economic powers, states, transnational corporations and financial institutions. Torture and other forms of inhumanity are still rampant. The apartheid system in South Africa continues its defiant, oppressive course.

The excesses of consumer waste are often revealed in patterns of exploitation of people and depletion of resources. The environment is still polluted without sufficient thought for the consequences. 'Small' wars are still being fought with tragic consequences. Militarism still dominates many societies. The problems of refugees continue. Political and religious fanaticisms violate human rights and freedoms. All forms of discrimination persist against women, ethnic religious and racial groups, indigenous peoples and marginalized sections of society.

As people of religion we ask what we can do to preserve the changes that have improved the human condition and to address those problems that remain. Human greed, self interest and pride will not disappear just by a change of the century. We must keep alive the conviction that the achievement of human happiness and fulfilment is dependent upon higher spiritual powers, powers which enable us to believe that peace is possible.

As people of religion we have responded to a call to build peace through trust. We realize that there are many definitions of trust. Therefore we must first break down the walls of mistrust. For us trust is active. We must acknowledge the manifold causes of mistrust that beset us as individuals, as peoples, even as religions. When we ask what creates fear in others we sometimes forget that the fears of others may stem from our insecurities and fears, our greed and selfishness, our striving for power and possession, our arrogance and ignorance.

We are sustained by a spiritual trust – our belief in the creative forces within the universe by which we are given life, in which we find beauty, by which we perceive truth, by which we live in hope. That spiritual trust is liberating and enabling. It is based on our living in harmony with the sources of our being, with other humans and with all of nature.

How then do we build peace through trust?

1. We build trust through disarmament and through the strengthening of institutions for conflict resolution. This kind of trust implies risk and vulnerability, because it depends on acceptance of mutual dependence rather than a reliance on mutual terror. In the field of disarmament, however, the recent development gives us hope that further progress can be made by reducing intercontinental ballistic missiles by 50%; stopping all nuclear weapons tests; banning the production and use of biological and chemical weapons; reducing conventional arms and arms trade; and adoption of a comprehensive programme of disarmament, including eliminating all nuclear weapons, by the year 2000.

To facilitate this process we have to develop confidence-building measures by broadening zones of peace and nuclear free zones; by preventing an arms race in outer space; by converting from military to civilian economy: and by shifting military-based research to peace-oriented research. In this way, the resources used for military purposes may be directed towards social, beneficial use and thus disarmament and development can be linked.

We recognize the role of the United Nations as one of the most effective conflict-resolution structures in the light of its recent achievements and want to help strengthen its role through our co-operation with it. At the same time, in its capacity as a religious non-governmental organization at the United Nations, WCRP has to serve all the more actively as an instrument of reconciliation wherever it is possible particularly in those situations in which religious issues and forces contribute to the conflict. In this context we would welcome the convening of an International Conference on the Middle East under United Nations auspices.

2. We build trust through the protection and preservation of human rights for all peoples. This kind of trust implies responsibility, a readiness to be accountable for the well-being of all, particularly those who are powerless or marginalized in our societies.

Women and children are the most vulnerable groups in our societies. Forced labour, drug usage and sexual exploitation all provide examples of the denial and degradation of their basic human rights. They are the first victims of war and they constitute over 80% of the present 13.5 million refugees. Because of these problems, we reaffirm our support for the efforts of the UN High Commissioner for Refugees, and the UN Development Fund for Women. We also support efforts to conclude the UN Convention on the Rights of the Child.

The rapid decimation of indigenous peoples and of their unique cultures go hand in hand with the degradation of our environment. Because of this plight, we strive for the speedy and full adoption of the Draft UN Declaration of Indigenous Rights.

Moral duty impels all people of faith to work for a greater justice. Warring political ideologies still curtail religious freedom in many countries. Religious fanaticism and intolerance only serve further to fuel insecurities. These struggles threaten world security. Often conflicts have both religious and political components as in the Sudanese, the Afghan, the Israeli-Palestinian and the South African cases. We must seek non-violent resolution of these struggles. In this regard, we are grateful for the effective role played by the UN and its peace-keeping forces. We also rejoice at the fortieth anniversary of the Universal Declaration of Human Rights and we call on our respective faith communities to join in this celebration. The growing trust shown in the United Nations family of organizations gives us hope for the future.

3. We build trust by the creation of economic systems that provide for and assure the well-being of all and that conserve and respect the ecological balances of nature. This kind of trust implies that we are the inheritors of a bountiful nature of which we are the stewards, to protect it, share it and pass on to our children and their children in wholeness.

Economic systems must be measured by ethical criteria, by how justly they provide for the well-being of all members of society, and by how they respect and use the environmental base that sustains all life.

Current economic systems do not measure well, as reflected in the ever widening gap between the rich and the poor, the burden of debt which impacts every society; the exploitation of human and natural resources located in some countries which supports the affluence and technological growth of other countries; and the massive displacement of population caught up in rural-urban migration.

We renew the long-standing hope for the creation of a new international economic order, assuring more equitable distribution of goods and services and greater participation in decision-making by the people.

Aware that economic and political structures are often intertwined with the religious structures of society, we call on the world's religious communities to examine their links to the power structures, and their own economic activity.

Our religious traditions agree that nature is to be respected. We are both trustees of nature and dependent upon it. Evidence abounds regarding the abuse and degradation of our global environment. We have polluted the oceans with toxic waste, and cut down forests for short term gain or to make way for industrial land usage. These and other careless uses of our resources have resulted both in the greenhouse effect and the depletion of the ozone layer.

Realizing that the condition of our common future will be determined by our current environmental and industrial practices, we call for increasing global consciousness of environmental issues. Our technological research should be directed toward the progressive upgrading of a sustainable global ecosystem. Long range planning for waste disposal, reforestation, and the conservation of non-renewable resources should be advocated and quickly implemented. We will indeed be held accountable for our stewardship of the inheritance we are to pass on to all living beings in the twenty-first century.

4. We build trust by educating ourselves and our children for peace, and through the use of non-violent methods of change and conflict resolution. This kind of trust we see as the confidence that comes when we know who we are and when we know others and reverence their human dignity, thereby overcoming the fear of the unknown, the fear of weakness, the stigma of difference.

Non-violence is love and love is the most powerful force against injustice and violence. Readiness to suffer for truth and justice can be an effective non-violent action. The use or threat of violence destroys trust. Hatred and the misuse of anger are forms of violence. There can be no building of peace where violence is involved. The roots of violence lie in the human condition. Therefore, the cultivation of non-violent behaviour, not only in our spiritual witness, but also through challenging media portrayals of enemies and glorification of violence, are necessary steps for peace and trust.

We need to challenge patterns of education which perpetuate prejudices and stereotypes, those in our text books, our religious teachings, our political rhetoric, wherever we focus on violence as power, prestige and solution. Since "history" is often shaped by the powerful, we should recognize that the difficulty of oppressed peoples to escape from 'unjust histories' destroys their ability to trust.

Religious communities and religious leaders can assist in global education, promoting positive learning experiences related to peoples of other cultures and other religions, in shaping their own religious curriculum, and in monitoring those patterns of behaviour that strengthen strong and loving family relations which provide the context for trans-formative social behaviour.

Conclusion

'Lead us from fear to trust.' Lead us from common terror to common security as we surrender our reliance on armaments, accept and love our enemies. Lead us from casualness to responsibility as we recognize in the suffering of others our oneness in the human family. Lead us from greed and selfishness to compassionate service as we acknowledge that the inheritance of the earth and all creation is not only to us, but to others and all succeeding generations. Lead us from ignorance to knowledge, from violence to non-violence as we learn of one another, as we overcome our suspicions, as we grow in patience and the ability to love and as we ourselves experience the inward peace.

2. Commission I: Building Trust Through Disarmament and Conflict Resolution Structures

Disarmament, international security and the relationship between disarmament and development

Regional and religious conflicts and conflict-resolution structures

The commission was cheered by the improvements in international relations since the last meeting of WCRP in 1984. 'Arms reduction can occur without a serious erosion of security, prolonged conflicts can be resolved, substantive work can be done on the relationship between development and disarmament' (p. 5). It was recognized that there were still major tasks ahead.

The continuance of nuclear weapon testing was deplored, there was a call for a nuclear freeze. There was a call for added support for the UN and for nations to observe their treaty obligations. There was an important stress on the role of NGOs (Non-governmental Organizations). It was suggested that WCRP could be more active in seeking reconciliation in areas of conflict. There was renewed concern about the effects of proselytizing.

The Role of NGOs

'We implore the NGO community, including religious organizations, to take more seriously their obligations resulting from UN accreditation. We note in particular the importance of NGO representation on a regular basis at both UN headquarters and the UN offices in Geneva and elsewhere' (pp. 8–9).

Conflict Resolution

'The Commission calls on the International Council to appoint Reconciliation Commissions or *ad hoc* groups to focus on specific areas of conflict in order to determine what WCRP could contribute to their solution . . . WCRP should take an initiative towards reconciliation in areas of conflict' (p. 10).

Religious Conflicts

'The Commission welcomes and supports the work of the UN for the protection of religious liberty, in particular the UN Declaration on the Elimination of All Forms of Intolerance and of Discrimination Based on Religion or Belief.

The Commission urges the International Council to draft a code of ethical conduct which would give guidelines on the protection of religious liberty as well as defining more closely inappropriate proselytizing and undue economic or social pressure' (p. 10).

3. Commission II: Building Trust Through Human Rights and Responsibility in the Family and Global Community

Human rights and responsibility in the family – for women, children, aged and spouses

Human rights and responsibility in the global community, political/social discrimination and oppression, minority protection and apartheid

The Commission in recalling recent world-wide celebrations of the fortieth anniversary of the UN Declaration on Human Rights recognized the 'unique indebtedness we owe to the relatively young UN institution' (p. 110). There are sections on The Rights of the Child, The Rights of Women, The Rights of Prisoners, Public Responsibilities, The Rights of Refugees. There are also proposals for action and special recommendations on the Middle East, on South Africa and on indigenous peoples.

The UN

'The UN has served as a common world platform enabling nations of the world to initiate the first steps in building peace through trust: the willingness to meet on an equal level. Similarly, WCRP has provided a world platform enabling religious people of the world to meet face to face on equal terms . . . We therefore stress the special vital link which the UN and WCRP share in their vision for a peaceful world' (p. 11).

The Rights of the Child

'Beyond stressing the crucial role which the family plays in protecting children, children's rights need international protection. We have to provide for the survival and development of children everywhere to protect them from harm and exploitation such as sexual abuse, homelessness, drugs, militarism, etc.'* (p. 11).

The Rights of Women

'We urge WCRP to publicize in all its national chapters the inhuman practice of trafficking in women from developing countries to developed countries. Frequently holding invalid or false passports, these women become virtual slaves . . .

We recommend the use of responsible family planning according to methods acceptable from the religious and medical points of view so as to avoid the greater problem of abortion' (pp. 11–12).

The Rights of Prisoners

'We express concern for psychiatric treatment of patients and prisoners which destroy human dignity, such as electric shock treatments and the use of certain drugs' (p. 12).

Public Responsibilities

'We express our concern about the effects on all people, especially the young, of advertising related to smoking and alcohol. We thus recommend that WCRP chapters urge their governments to curb such advertising.'

The Rights of Refugees

'Since women and children constitute more than 80% of the current 13.5 million refugees, we express our deep concern about the plight of refugees and displaced persons in particular in South Asia, Africa and Central America. We stress their rights of resettlement, family reunion, employment, education and cultural restoration' (p. 12).

4. Commission III: Building Trust Through Economic and Social Development and Ecological Balance

This report is remarkably specific in its comments on economic and ecological issues, especially on Third World debt. It tries to apply moral judgments to these issues and makes clear recommendations as to the action that individual believers can take.

* Prior to the adoption of the UN Convention on the Rights of the Child, WCRP with UNICEF arranged a conference on The World's Religions for the World's Children. See below, pp. 143ff.

Economic and Social Development, new international economic order and development assistance

Economic and Social Situation of the world

'The present international economic order is based mostly on greed and profit making, not on morals, justice and love as our various religions proclaim' (p. 16).

Debt

'The debts of the developing countries are in large measure an unjust burden placed on them by the developed countries, and have become a source of misery for them. From an economic and moral point of view this has occurred because of the removal of resources by the countries holding the debts. Therefore, there is no obligation to pay back the debts because the amount involved has already been taken from the countries in the form of resources belonging to the indebted countries' (p. 16).

Responsibilities of religious bodies in the present economic situation

'We suggest the situation can be approached in the following ways.

(a) As members of the major religions of the world, we have to reconsider the fact that many religious institutions are part of the economic powers of the present world. They contribute to unjust economic relations.

(b) As believers, each of us is responsible for the improvement of the economic order within our own community as well as bearing responsibility for the worsening of this same order. That means we all bear part of the responsibility for the contemporary unjust economic order.

(c) The question is what can we do as individuals and as organized bodies for the purpose of improving this economic and social situation' (p. 17).

Action Proposals for WCRP

(a) ... 'The present economic order of the world is unjust ...' (p. 17).

(b) 'WRCP should appeal to the conscience of governments and religious leaders to fight corruption and mismanagement ...' (p. 18).

(c) 'WCRP should invite all religious people to act together and support measures to eradicate the debts of developing countries as a moral duty to humanity' (p. 18).

Resolutions

'1. We resolve that WCRP members be encouraged to support existing tax resistance movements in countries where this matter of conscience is organized against military and armament expenses' (p. 18)

Ecological Balance and Human Environment

Humanity and Nature

'All religions agree that nature is to be respected. This traditional respect has been abused and misrepresented to justify destruction of nature. Yet it remains true that all faiths see humanity as both trustee and dependent upon nature' (p. 19).

Many negative developments are listed and the commission called upon followers of all faiths to take action against the profiteer responsible.

'Religions are a source of vision and progress, strength, restraint of greed, compassion, unity of all humanity, unity of nature and humanity, inspiration and encouragement to act collectively and with trust.

Peace requires harmony and balance, world renewal replacing the old order, decent living standards for all, without excess for some; it also requires that community be based on spirit, in which there be enough for everyone's need and not for everyone's greed, as Gandhi has said.

If technology is to be beneficial it must not be based on economic theory of growth, but be based on green, clean, indigenous ways, use non-violent, non-capital destructive technology, not promote maximum consumption, be use-oriented, rather than invent new human needs' (p. 20).

Principles for action

(a) Changes in individual life style and education.

(b) Decentralization: locally based, small-scale projects such as tree nurseries, village development, grass roots, bottom-up organizations.

(c) World-wide interreligious personal networking which promotes religious reflections on the theme of life and its value, facilitating easier access to information about the view of all religions on life and nature.

(d) Long term planning which respects the long term truth that ecological planning is also profitable.

Proposals

'Recognizing that consumerism is based on violence', each member of WCRP was urged to give up at least one convenience so as to set an example of simple living (p. 20).

Each member was urged 'to explore his or her own tradition's contribution to a philosophy/spirituality/theology of ecology' and to 'engage in dialogue on the contribution of religious thought to the question of ecology and the survival of the planet' (p. 21).

5. Commission IV: Building Trust Through Non-Violence and Education for Peace

This report examines the religious motivation for trust, which is seen as a freedom from fear and an openness to others, and it looks at the obstacles which prevent trust. It makes useful suggestions about ways of building trust. The report also gives the strongest endorsement so far in WCRP literature of the way of non-violence and looks at the spiritual resources necessary. It makes clear that non-violence is a power for change, not passive acquiescence in injustice.

The religious motivation for trust

'There are central motivations for human trust, rooted in the understanding of life taught in our religious traditions. The Golden Rule – "Do unto others as you would have them do to you" – is a common code for trust used by all religious people. Dependence upon the spiritual dimension in our respective religions is felt to be essential to lead us into solidarity and trust with all people and all nature.

We are thankful that motivated and inspired by our religious teachings, we can try to practise trust within our communities, but we are calling upon ourselves to expand that trust to reach out to others in families, society and in the global community.'

Obstacles that prevent trust

The lack of trust between religious communities was admitted. It was recognized that unjust history destroys the ability to trust. Where majorities dominate minorities trust is destroyed.

'Misunderstandings, prejudices and injustice have been the breeding ground of mistrust.

Exposure to violent and pornographic images in the media destroy trust in relationships between men and women and between peoples.

The lack of balance between religious and moral aspects in education has led to a lack of emphasis on building trust in the educational system' (pp. 22–3).

Ways of Building Trust

'(a) Being with and listening to people, particularly where they suffer injustice and deprivation, helping them to overcome their mistrust and building up their confidence, educating them where they are . . .

(b) Allowing suffering peoples to speak of their suffering and be helped to understand the unjust structures which cause them to suffer can build trust.

(c) Knowledge can be a liberating factor.

(d) Religious, aesthetic and moral emphasis in education is a positive contribution to trust. Education can be a positive force for building trust' (p. 23).

Non-violence

'Non-violence should not be passive but positive, active and dynamic. Non-violence is love and love is the most powerful force against evil and violence. How can people be helped to be non-violent? Where do we start? With ourselves, realizing that this can only come from the depth of our religious experience. To practise non-violence we need to be completely free from fear, willing to accept the full consequences of our stance. We have to be free from all anger and hatred. Hatred is itself a form of violence' (p. 23).

Self-renewal

'Personal self-renewal means coming to terms with anger, learning how to confront in love the cause of anger through prayer and constant offering of the person to the Supreme Power. Only with the help of this Supreme Power can the way of non-violence be achieved' (p. 23).

Commitment to Change

'Non-violence is an active force of the highest order . . . It is the courage to face violent situations non-violently which makes non-violence effective. We must be positively concerned to achieve change non-violently and not passively acquiescing in evil' (p. 24).

The power of love

'Love is the most powerful force against evil and violence . . . There can be no building peace through trust where violence is involved. The roots of violence lie in the human mind. Humans need to be able to tap the positive energy from their souls and become embodiments of love, peace and trust in a deep relationship with the Supreme Power' (p. 25).

Education

There is again stress on the need for education for peace and interfaith understanding.

'We appeal to all religious leaders to promote interfaith dialogue and cooperation among theologians and religious education at all levels . . . and to monitor text books and other educational material, and particularly to avoid and eliminate negative stereotypes' (p. 25).

Declarations of the International Association for Religious Freedom

The International Association for Religious Freedom was founded in 1900. It consists of more than fifty-eight member groups in twenty-two countries, on all continents. Member groups may be of any religion or may be inter-religious in composition. An International Congress is held every three years, attended by individuals who belong to member groups and by invited experts. A declaration is usually approved by the Congress and published. Some are quite general in tone, others make specific recommendations. Three recent declarations are reproduced here.

I   The IARF Manifesto on the World Community

The IARF Manifesto on the World Community was endorsed by the Twenty-Second Congress of the International Association for Religious Freedom (IARF) in Montreal, from 15–21 August 1975.

Long-Term Goals

We believe that we should strive to achieve the following five long-term goals as a minimum by the end of the century; so as to provide at least a basis for a more humane and just world community:

1. *Peace*. The present arms race is both too dangerous and too expensive to be tolerated in a nuclear age. We advocate: (*a*) the minimization of large-scale collective violence by the year 2000 by means of a phased programme leading toward general and complete disarmament; (*b*) the elimination of all national military capabilities; (*c*) the creation of an international police force; and (*d*) the development of machinery for adjudicating disputes and correcting injustices.

2. *Economic well-being*. We find it unconscionable that at a time of un-surpassed affluence for hundreds of millions of people, there are even larger numbers who live below any conceivable level of human dignity. We

advocate a combination of trade, aid, population and resource policies which will permit all people in all countries to enjoy the basic necessities of life by the year 2000. This includes, at a minimum, the right to food, shelter, health, economic security and a basic education. We further advocate measures ensuring a shift from the currently widening gap between developed and developing countries to a substantial closing of this gap.

This overall goal will entail, among other things: (*a*) a massive transfer of resources and technology from the developed to the developing countries; (*b*) allocating aid by objective criteria of need; (*c*) revamping of internal economic policies to ensure that the benefits of development are widely dispersed among the entire population; (*d*) a massive attack on the soaring rates of population growth; (*e*) drastically revised trade policies to ensure stable and fair prices for the products of the poorer countries; and (*f*) the regulation of transnational corporations so that their actions do not defeat the development policies of the countries where they operate.

3. *Freedom from oppression.* Historically, the Socialist countries have emphasized economic rights and well-being while the Western industrialized countries have championed political and civil rights. We hold that a unified and harmonious world community demands that *both* types of rights be upheld in all countries. We have specified basic economic rights in the previous section. Here we uphold the rights of all persons to freedom of expression and political choice in all countries. Adequate international machinery must be devised not only to define such rights (as the UN has done) but to implement them effectively.

Along with these basic political rights, we believe that by the year 2000 the world community should achieve the goal of ensuring the end of colonialism, the replacement of regimes imposing minority rule on members of different ethnic groups, and such gross violations of human rights as the practice of torture and political imprisonment.

International human rights machinery should also move aggressively to eliminate gross patterns of discrimination based on race, sex or other invidious distinctions. As religious liberals, we are particularly concerned that the world community ensure the right to religious freedom.

6. *Ecological integrity.* As the world moved from a gross global product (GGP) of one trillion dollars in 1950 to three trillion dollars in 1970, the stresses on the ecosystem suddenly mushroomed. Lakes atrophied, oil spills multiplied, the fish catch fell off for the first time, and devastating floods from deforestation occurred more and more frequently. If the world moves on to a widely forecast level of a ten trillion dollar GGP by the end of the century, it can be expected that the amount of pollution and the number of eco-catastrophes will mount at an expanding rate. We advocate that by the year 2000 the current deterioration in the ecosystem be halted and that a high level of ecological quality be maintained indefinitely. We further

advocate the close monitoring of scarce resources, so that they can be conserved to meet the needs of future generations.

We also advocate that the wasteful consumption patterns of the developed countries be moderated, and that the populations of these countries be stabilized with the same high priority which is urged on the developing countries, since each person in an affluent society causes many more times as much pollution and uses up far more of the world's scarce resources.

5. *World governance*. We advocate that the United Nations be given the funds and authority which are necessary to achieve the above named goals effectively. Today, the General Assembly may only make recommendations and the Security Council has been virtually immobilized. Authority is needed, for instance, to regulate transnational pollution, to ensure that disarmament agreements are carried out, to implement basic human rights, to regulate the conduct of multinational corporations, and to conserve scarce resources. Authority is also needed if the massive funds needed for economic well-being are to be raised on an equitable basis from all countries.

As funding and authority are added to the various United Nations operations, the organization will move in the direction of becoming a true world government instead of a forum for discussing possible voluntary cooperation by governments with often diverse and conflicting interests and objectives. We advocate building a worldwide ethos favourable to such a transformation to a true world government – a government capable of creating and enforcing world law. Assuming such an ethos is developed, we favour the creation of a world legislature, whose members are directly elected by the peoples of the world, dispute-adjudicating mechanisms, and a series of executive departments built upon the basis of the existing specialized agencies. Because we favour the maximum limitation of political power to achieve the goals of a united world community, we urge that this government be given no more authority than is strictly necessary to accomplish its basic tasks effectively.

We see these five goals as inextricably interdependent. The peace for which we yearn is a peace of wholeness – a peace in which no nation is driven to violence because of unjust treatment, a peace free of fear of nuclear holocaust or threat of ecological catastrophe, a peace in which all are free to strive toward self-fulfilment and joy and harmony, a peace of mutual trust, respect and concern.

II The Twenty-Fifth Congress of the International Association for Religious Freedom (IARF Japan Congress), held in Tokyo in 1984

The Peace to which we Aspire

We recognise that peace has both an inner, spiritual aspect, 'peace of mind', and an external aspect expressed as 'peace on earth'. These two must be inseparable.

'Peace of mind' is a peace which issues from harmony among individuals, the harmony between humankind and nature, the unity of humankind and truth, and the unity between the human family and God – a peace which exists in the human heart.

'Peace on earth' refers not just to the absence of war and conflict, but is a peace of wholeness (as declared in the IARF Montreal Manifesto of 1975) in which people are free from hunger, poverty, aggression and discrimination, and in which human dignity, freedom, equality, and justice are realized.

Spiritual peace is the foundation for peace in the world. In order to establish true peace we must start from the foundation of inner peace. This peace is intimately connected to social and cultural factors, and true peace can be attained only through social systems which link people with people, societies with societies, and nations with nations.

We believe that God is present among all people, and all human beings possess conscience and reason.

We believe that truth and love are the uniting forces behind freedom, justice and peace.

We believe that there can be no true victor where hostility is met with hostility, and violence is countered with violence. Therefore hostility must be met with forgiveness, and violence with the power of truth and love.

We believe that within the variety of manifestations all religions speak of one ultimate reality.

We are deeply aware that it is the responsibility of people of religion to search for reconciliation and unity for the peoples of the world.

We, as religious people, will not be content simply to expound the principles of peace. In order actually to bring about peace, we must exert all our energy to work together with all people to achieve these ideals and purposes.

We declare that in this nuclear age a peace based on the balance of military power is an illusion which leads to destruction, and that the way to peace is the path of diplomacy and non-violence.

We affirm the spirit of the Japanese Constitution, which forever renounces the use of military force. This noble ideal ought to be preserved and promoted among all nations.

We note that the current prosperity of Japan is due, in part, to the fact that because war has been renounced, valuable resources have not been spent on military expenditures, but have been transferred to the improvement of the welfare of society.

We appeal urgently to the leaders of each country to put the good of the whole human family above national self-interest, which easily becomes idolatry. We call on them to banish all nuclear weapons, and to promote energetically the absolute reduction of all kinds of armaments. We insist that the vast sums of money spent on military expenditures be used to promote peace and human welfare.

We appeal urgently to the industrialized countries and to the United Nations to increase their support for the developing countries in order to help them overcome hunger and poverty, and to promote vigorously measures to establish a more just international economic order.

We also appeal urgently to the leaders of each nation to implement the Universal Declaration of Human Rights and the international covenants on human rights.

We call for the establishment of a more humane educational system which is directed toward the restoration of human dignity and with emphasis on spiritual values.

Action Programme for Peace

We desire earnestly that the IARF, its member groups, and individuals accept, apply, and promote the following proposals in cooperation with religious leaders around the world in whatever way is most suitable in their particular situations:

1. Pray for peace with justice;
2. Diligently carry out self-discipline and practices necessary to reform one's own group, based on such religious values as truth, love, sincerity, freedom, justice, and peace;
3. Promote mutual understanding and cooperation among all religions and peoples, including exchange programmes;
4. Appeal to the government of each country to abolish nuclear weapons, reduce armaments, and promote policies which support human rights, the equality of women, development, and the elimination of hunger;
5. Encourage all governments to observe the Charter of the United Nations, implement the Final Document of the 1978 Special Session on Disarmament, and strengthen procedures for the peaceful settlement of disputes;
6. Cooperate with people in all walks of life to promote the UN World Disarmament Campaign and other movements to halt the arms race and to promote human rights, development, and peace.
7. Undertake special activities for the International Year of Peace (1986).

8. Promote, through research and education, the renewal of true humanness, the philosophy of peace, and the spiritual development of youth;

9. Support efforts being made for a worldwide gathering of religions under the combined auspices of the leaders of various world religions in order to develop strategies for extricating ourselves from the crises facing humankind.

Within less than twenty years humankind will enter the twenty-first century. Whether we will follow the road to life and bliss or will walk the way to darkness and destruction is the choice which humanity will make.

We religious people hold in our hands the heavy responsibility of showing the way which humankind should choose in order to attain life and blessings, and hereby we declare that we will strive with all our physical and spiritual strength to accomplish this noble task.

From the depths of our hearts we are praying that under the guidance of the Most High the day of unity and peace for the human family will come quickly.

III The Twenty-Seventh Assembly of the International Association for Religious Freedom, held in Hamburg, Federal Republic of Germany, in 1990

Concerns

Our Study Groups have identified specific issues for concern and action. We call attention to the following broad concerns:

First and foremost is an overarching hope for peace. The imperative for disarmament seems self-evident, involving reductions in both production and sale of arms. Peace is not only absence of conflict, but the dream of one world living cooperatively, valuing the rich diversity of the human community.

Peace both within states and between states cannot be sustained without social justice. Society has an obligation to provide conditions for the full development of all members of our fellow human family. It is unacceptable that some live in opulence, hundreds of millions of our fellow human beings are perpetually hungry, or that every year tens of millions die of starvation or easily preventable diseases. It is equally unacceptable that part of a nation's people suffer the daily humiliations of poverty, while fellow citizens ignore their sufferings in the pursuit of even greater wealth.

Intolerance and fanaticism breed hatred which provides a potential power for destruction. The consequences of such hatred were brought forcefully to our minds and hearts in a visit to Neate, a former concentration camp.

Our abuse of the natural and animal world is alarming: acid rain, damage to the ozone layer, massive pollution of the environment by chemical and nuclear waste, and cruel practices in scientific research and animal farming demand our attention and change in life patterns.

Recommendations

As individuals and member groups
We share with our groups in our home countries the resolutions and recommendations made here.
IARF take active steps to work for religious cooperation and interfaith dialogue.
Member groups will work for the maximum numbers of states becoming parties to international human rights conventions including: the Covenant on Civil and Political Rights and its Optional Protocol; the Convention on the Elimination of all forms of Discrimination Against Women; the Convention Against Racism; the Convention Against Torture and the Convention on the Rights of the Child.
Member groups will also inform themselves of the work of the United Nations Commission on Human Rights and its Sub-Commission.

6

Declaration on the Oneness of
The Human Family

The Temple of Understanding was founded in 1960 by Judith Hollister. It has drawn together interested individuals from all faiths who seek understanding and unity. Some distinguished religious leaders have attended these meetings. A series of Spiritual Summit Conferences have been held. At the sixth such conference held in New York in 1984, a 'Declaration on the Oneness of the Human Family' was adopted. This had been drafted by Dr Robert Muller, who was then Assistant Secretary General of the United Nations.

Declaration on the Oneness of The Human Family

Adopted at Spiritual Summit Conference VI, in 1984

A convergence of world religions towards a 'Global Spirituality' might suggest the following points in common:

1. The Oneness of the Human Family, irrespective of colour, sex, creed, nation or any other distinctive characteristic.
2. The harmonious place of the individual person in the total order of things, as a unique entity of Divine Origin, with a basic relationship to the Universe and Eternity.
3. The Importance of spiritual exercises, meditation, prayer, contemplation, and the inner search as links between human life and the universe.
4. The Existence of an incipient conscience at the heart of humanity which speaks for what is good and against what is bad for the human family; which advocates and fosters understanding, co-operation and altruism instead of division, struggle and indifference among nations.
5. The value of Dedicated Service to others, with a compassionate response to human suffering, with special attention to the oppressed and the poor, the handicapped and the elderly, the rejected and the lonely.
6. The Duty to give thanks and express gratitude for the abundance of life which has been given to humanity, an abundance not to be selfishly possessed or accumulated, but to be shared and given generously to

those who are in need, with a respect for human dignity and a sense of social justice.

7. The need for Ecumenical agencies and World Religious organizations to foster dialogue and collaborative arrangements, and to bring the resources and inspirations of the religions to bear upon the solution of world problems.

8. A rejection of violence as being contrary to the sanctity and uniqueness of life and a total acceptance of the precept – 'Thou shalt not kill'.

9. An affirmation of the law of Love and Compassion as the great transcending force which alone can break the nemesis of war and establish a Planet of Peace.

10. The Evolutionary task of human life and society to move through the eternal stream of time towards interdependence, communion, and an ever expanding realization of Divinity.

7

The Mt Abu Declaration

In April 1988 people of goodwill, of many races and cultural backgrounds, of many religions, from north, south, east and west, launched 'Global Co-operation for a Better World'. The initiative was taken by the Brahma Kumaris and was welcomed by the United Nations and world leaders, and professionals and community leaders from many nations. It was the successor to 'A Million Minutes of Peace', the largest worldwide, non-fundraising project of the International Year of Peace in 1986.

The response was enthusiastic. Millions of people became involved. Global Co-operation gave them the opportunity to express their own personal vision of a better world, individually and collectively, and then encouraged them to implement their vision in action, thus affirming their belief in the worth and the dignity of the human being.

In February 1989, leaders from over forty countries, key figures in the project, gathered together in Mount Abu, Rajastan, India, at the Headquarters of the Brahma Kumaris World Spiritual University for the Mount Abu Summit on Global Co-operation.

Having received reports from sixty countries, including the hopes and visions for a better world contained in the Global Co-operation Bank, they reached certain conclusions recorded in this statement.

This statement was addressed to world leaders and to the people of the world as a basis for co-operation at every level of human endeavour.

A presentation of the Declaration was made at the Dag Hammarskjold Auditorium of the United Nations in May 1989.

The Mt Abu Declaration 1989

As a global family we share the same unique planet and share the same hopes and aspirations for a just and humane world. Yet, as we approach the dawn of the next millennium, we are concerned that life on earth is threatened.

Our beautiful planet is faced with a crisis of unprecedented magnitude.

In many cultures, the moral fabric of society is challenged by violence, crime, addiction, denial of human rights and human dignity, and the disintegration of family life.

At the same time, we, the people of the world, are yearning for peace and a better world for ourselves and our children. How is it, that with all the human skill and talent that exists, with all the achievements in technology, there is still grinding poverty, massive arms expenditure and a grave deterioration in the enviroment?

There is so much to be done and so many willing hands and hearts to do it. What is needed is the spirit of co-operation and goodwill, the attitude of love and respect towards each other, the practice of positive and creative thinking, the application of moral and spiritual values in daily life, as well as action based on a shared vision of a better world.

Now is the time to call on the will and the clear vision of the people:

> 'A vision without a task is but a dream
> A task without a vision is a drudgery
> A vision with a task
> can change the world.'

The voice of the people must be heard. This Declaration is an acknowledgement that it is the people who, by their active participation and co-operation, can change the world.

The Peoples' Vision

From the personal and group 'visions' already received by the Global Co-operation Bank in sixty countries, the picture of a better world has begun to take shape. Based on an analysis of these inputs, the sort of world in which people would like to live includes the following characteristics:

1. There would be reverence for life.
2. There would be recognition of, and respect for, the dignity and integrity of every human being.
3. The environment would be clean, fresh and green, and in a state of ecological balance. There would be a sustainable relationship between population and resources.
4. Every human being would be healthy and content in spirit, mind and body.
5. Every human being would have shelter, food and water.
6. All individuals would be at peace with themselves.
7. There would be social, economic and political justice, as well as respect for human rights.

8. There would be love, trust, friendship and understanding in all human relationships.
9. Family life would be loving and fulfilling, and would contribute to the sense of the universal family living in harmony.
10. All individuals would have equal opportunities for growth, educational progress and employment, with full encouragement to develop all their potentialities.
11. Every individual would enjoy freedom of expression, movement and action, whilst respecting the liberties and rights of others.
12. There would be open and frank communication at all levels of society.
13. There would be honesty and a sense of responsibility within governing bodies in all sectors of society.
14. There would be the commitment of governments to work for the welfare and advancement of people.
15. There would be co-operation at local, national and international levels.

This vision of a better world will continue to evolve as more and more people contribute their 'visions' to the Global Co-operation Bank.

The Principles of Co-operation

As participants at the Mt Abu Summit, we have identified the following basic Principles of Co-operation which contribute towards the achievement and sustainability of effective co-operation at any level:
1. In any endeavour the hopes, needs and common goals of those concerned are clearly identified and communicated.
2. Co-operation between individuals and groups is a voluntary process based on tolerance, understanding, mutual benefit and respect.
3. In every endeavour there is a sense of honesty and trust between partners in co-operation.
4. Recognizing the fundamental dignity of each human being, all rise above narrow considerations and work together in a spirit of harmony.
5. The process of co-operation is enhanced by the reduction of any tension through mental relaxation, positive thinking and quiet reflection.
6. The contribution of each person or group of people is considered integral to the accomplishment of any co-operative task.
7. There is individual and collective responsibility in any co-operative decisions and actions.
8. All listen and acknowledge the views and ideas of others in any co-operative task.

Therefore

We call on the people of the world to unite and co-operate with each other to create a better world.

We pledge our support for the principles and objectives of the United Nations.

We believe that the era of negative thinking and confrontation which has given rise to the arms race and the consequent waste of human and economic resources must end.

We must overcome apathy and inertia with courage and steadfast hope. In doing so, let us now, as instruments of peace, shape our own destiny and resolve to bring into reality a better world for all.

8

Declaration of Human Responsibilities for Peace and Sustainable Development

This declaration was agreed at a conference held in San José, Costa Rica in June 1989. It was co-hosted by the University for Peace, the Government of Costa Rica, the Catholic Church of Costa Rica and the University of Costa Rica. The participants, present as individuals, belonged to many religions and came from different parts of the world. Active participants were the Dalai Lama and Dr Oscar Arias Santiez, at the time President of Costa Rica.

The document was presented to the United Nations by the Government of Costa Rica.

See *World Faiths Insight*, New Series 23, October 1989, pp. 21–2.

Declaration of Human Responsibilities for Peace and Sustainable Development

Chapter I
The Unity of the World

Article 1:

Everything that exists is part of the unfolding of an interdependent universe. All beings belonging to this universe have a common origin and are pursuing concurrent evolutionary paths. Therefore, the evolution and development of all humanity and each human being is an integral part of the evolution of the universe.

Article 2:

All human beings belong inseparably to nature, upon which human culture and civilization have been constructed.

Article 3:

Life on Earth is abundant and diverse. It is sustained by the uninterrupted functioning of natural systems that ensure the supply of energy, air, water, and nutrients for all living beings, which depend upon one another and the rest of nature for their existence, well-being and development. Every manifestation of life on Earth is unique and necessary, and therefore is owed respect and care regardless of its apparent value to human beings.

Chapter II
The Unity of the Human Family

Article 4:

All human beings belong inseparably to the human family and depend on one another for existence, well-being, and development. Each human being is a unique expression and manifestation of life and has his or her own contributions to make to the development of life on Earth, irrespective of differences in race, colour, sex, language, religion, political or other opinion, national or social origin, economic or other status. Furthermore, each is the beneficiary of fundamental and inalienable rights and liberties.

Article 5:

All human beings have the same basic needs, and the same fundamental aspirations for their fulfilment. All individuals are the beneficiaries of the right to development, which seeks to promote the achievement of the full potential of each person.

Chapter III
Human Choices and Responsibility

Article 6:

Altruism, compassion and love are intrinsic qualities of all human beings. These qualities nurture responsibility, which is an inherent aspect of every relationship in which human beings are involved. This capacity to act responsibly, in a conscious, independent, unique and personal way, is an inalienable creative quality of each human being. There is no limit to its scope or depth other than that which each person establishes for him- or herself. The more it is accepted and exercised, the more it will grow and strengthen.

Article 7:

Of all living beings, humans have the unique capacity to decide consciously whether to protect or to damage the quality and conditions of life on Earth. By reflecting on their membership in the natural world and their special position as participants in the unfolding of natural processes, people can develop an altruistic sense of universal responsibility toward the world as a whole for the protection of nature, the promotion of the highest possible evolutionary potential, and for the creation of those conditions which allow for the achievement of the highest level of spiritual and material well-being.

Article 8:

At this critical point in history, human choices are crucial. In directing their actions towards achieving progress in society, human beings often have lost sight of their membership in the natural community and the indivisible human family, and their basic needs for a healthy life. Excessive consumption, abuse of the environment, and aggression among peoples have brought natural processes to a critical situation that threatens the Earth's survival. By reflecting on this, individuals will be able to discern their responsibility, and on this basis re-orient their conduct towards peace and sustainable development.

Chapter IV
A Reorientation Toward Peace and Sustainable Development

Article 9:

It is through the recognition that every form of life is unique and necessary, that every person is the beneficiary of the Right to development, and that peace and violence have their origins in the consciousness of human beings, that a conscious sense of responsibility to act and think in a peaceful manner will be developed. Through this peaceful consciousness, individuals will understand the nature of the conditions necessary for their well-being and development.

Article 10:

Conscious of their sense of responsibility towards the human family, the environment which they inhabit, and the necessity of thinking and acting peacefully, human beings will be obligated to act in a manner which is consistent both with the observance and respect of the inherent rights of people, and with the consumption of resources which are sustainable.

Article 11:

Upon recognizing that the members of the human family are responsible to themselves and to present and future generations for the conservation of the Earth, as protectors of the natural community and promoters of continued development, all people will pledge themselves to acting in a rational manner in order to achieve sustainable living.

Article 12:

States have the responsibility to promote peace and sustainability, as well as to put into practice the educational objectives that further them. These objectives include the awakening of the consciousness of the interdependence among human beings and between human beings and nature, and the universal responsibility of the individual to solve, through attitudes and actions, the problems which have been created, in a manner which is consistent with the protection of human rights and fundamental liberties.

9

International Conferences on Peace and Nonviolent Action

Two international conferences on Peace and Nonviolent Action have been held by the Anuvrat Movement, which is a Jain peace movement, led by His Holiness Acharya Tulsi. The first was held at Ladnum in Rajasthan, India, from 5 to 7 December 1988. This issued the 'Ladnun Declaration', which, because it includes a large number of detailed and quite specific recommendations, is worth reproducing in full, although the list of suggestions is daunting. There is little reference to existing attempts to achieve some of the objectives mentioned.

The Second International Conference was held at Rajsamand, India from 17 to 21 February 1991. Attached to the general statement, there is a useful outline of a Suggested Course for Training in Nonviolence.

1. Ladnun Declaration

Preamble

We the citizens of the world hailing from different countries who have assembled here in the idyllic surroundings of the Jain University campus to participate in this historic conference recognize that we have a common overriding goal of attaining peace through nonviolent action and realize that an action is fearful without direction and that once a direction is determined it is possible to make assertive and courageous endeavours towards accomplishing our cherished aspirations. We also believe that the lofty goal of eradicating all forms of violence that threaten the existence of mankind today cannot be realized unless a global campaign exhorting people to give their mite to the noble cause of peace by doing some actions is launched at individual, social, national and international levels. Guided by the spirit embodied in the above lines, we make the following recommendations and declare that their adoption by the institutions and individuals of the world will pave the way for the advent of a peaceful and nonviolent world.

1. Organizational

    (i)   Welcome PEACE in the midst of all peace gatherings.

(ii)   Use peace tableaux at such gatherings to clarify the conception of peace.

(iii)   Organize workshops, evaluations and follow-ups.

(iv)   Set up NGOs for peace, reinforcing existing organizations.

(v)   Establish centres for the training of peace brigades in nonviolence.

(vi)   Promote criss-cross networkings among peace organizations as well as amongst such institutions.

(vii)   Promote interchange of peace activities and organizations at personal level.

(viii)   Mobilize public opinion in favour of disarmament.

(ix)   Establish centres for dissemination of international information regarding peace and nonviolent action.

(x)   Stress unity and rights of all beings and prepare a list of principles leading to the framing of laws, even at the level of animal-citizenship-rights, to bring about equality among all beings in a nonviolent world.

(xi)   Stop acts of cruelty towards animals at all organizational levels and promote the cause of peace in public minds and especially children.

(xii)   Hold future conferences in areas of the world where there are problems activating potential violence.

2. Educational

(i)   Encourage studies, meditational training and research on international cooperation for peace and non-violent action.

(ii)   Follow up peace research histories and individual network of happenings to co-ordinate analysis and peace strategies.

(iii)   Encourage peace education through poetry, fine art, music, dance/drama and cultural exchanges.

(iv)   Include a study of the Human Rights Declaration and work towards its implementation.

(v)   Promote through the medium of the press the peace oriented programmes and notices.

(vi)   Include a study of the declaration of Children's rights and work towards its implementation.

(vii)   Take up a case study of the Nuremberg Principles against war and try to improve upon them in accordance with world peace principles by cross-references to the international laws of warfare.

(viii)   Undertake the study of the constitutions of various countries in order to realize how they undertake to follow fundamental rights, human rights and in what respect.

(ix)   Impart training in nonviolence at family level.

(x)   Learn and teach how to communicate well with others successfully.

(xi)   Teach positive resolution skills to children and young students.

(xii)   Include peace education in the curricula of the teacher-trainees as well as of the young students.
(xiii) Educate the children in peace activities and respect them.
(xiv)   Make available inspiring literature on peace and nonviolence.
(xv)   Arrange the teaching of history in the framework of nonviolence.
(xvi)   Foster a comparative study of religions so as to avoid religious wars and tensions and ensure lasting peace and happiness.
(xvii) Eliminate biases of nationalism inherent in the present system.
(xviii) Include peace education in the global academic curriculums.
(xix)   Find new systems of curriculums to counterbalance methods of training in violence presently being used.
(xx)   Initiate steps for establishing world interfaith schools and colleges for promoting global education.

3. Global Action

(i)   Start an international transcultural peace pledge chain.
(ii)   Establish a non-governmental united organization of the people which may be named United Peoples' Organization for establishing sovereignty of PEACE and NON-VIOLENCE.
(iii)   Send and depute NGO representatives to UNO and its specialized agencies.
(iv)   Create a People's Parliament for Peace and Nonviolent Action in every country.
(v)   Substitute (and supply) nonviolent Defence Structures for violent means of national defence structures.
(vi)   Impress upon the Press, Police, Politicians and Judiciary the obligation to uphold the supremacy of peace and nonviolence and to respect the true principles of law and order in that context.
(vii)   Recommend and press for making a separate Ministry of Peace and Nonviolence in every country.

4. Social Action

(i)   Assist the present social service organizations to bring honour and dignity to the individuals.
(ii)   Support one another in peace activities.
(iii)   Entertain resolutions of conflicts and dispose of them immediately.
(iv)   Put up non-cooperation with militarized defence structures in this era of Nuclear Armaments in the members' own country when morally called upon.
(v)   Promote nonviolent defence and social defence methods, that is civilian defence as opposed to military defence.
(vi)   Involve children in peace processes as Ancillary Civil Force.
(vii)   Object to and protest against the violence presently exhibited in mass media.

(viii) Provide adequate primary training to the masses for civil disobedience against acts of violence, first by talks, lectures and visual media and then by token demonstrations at all levels of the social participation in the sacred cause of PEACE and NONVIOLENCE.
(ix) Ban/boycott the sale and purchase of war toys.
(x) Rehabilitate people who fall victims to violence and provide social openings for them.
(xi) Promote a way of life which is in tune with healthy living food habits (vegetarianism as an example), right conduct, everabiding love for peace and justice.

5. Individual Action

(i) Promote an inner awakening towards tolerance and coexistence in individuals.
(ii) Respect one another's views or path to peace and practically promote it more by personal involvement than by suggestions.
(iii) Tolerate and respect one another's point of view and innovate new ideas for peace.
(iv) Say 'No' to violence and 'Yes' to nonviolence for all.
(v) Promote nonviolent defence at individual levels.
(vi) Promote the voluntary limitations of wants and means.
(vii) Promote cleanliness and simplicity in attire and surroundings.
(viii) See that people don't use abusive language and abusive slang by way of talking or habit.
(ix) Promote hobbies in arts, crafts and music and adopt worldwide penfriendship and spend adequate time and means in involvement therein.
(x) Encourage writing frequent letters to editors and legislatures highlighting issues of violence and injustice in order to establish truth, nonviolence and justice.
(xi) Set examples of peace, love, nonviolence and moral conduct in life.
(xii) Pledge yourself to side with the underprivileged, the poor and the oppressed to check deprivation of needs and essentials.
(xiii) Expose disguises of bonded labour and recurring social evils at personal level.
(xiv) Eradicate drug abuse and alcoholism.
(xv) Check food wastage of every kind and see that poor men, animals, pets and birds are fed properly out of such supplies.
(xvi) Promote kitchen-gardening and pot-plant growing of vegetables as a way to promote a peace fund of food.
(xvii) Promote plantation of fruit-trees, medicinal plants and herbs as home to home dispensaries and healthy living.
(xviii) Encourage interested people to write one letter each day either inland or abroad with an intention to promote peace links and goodwill among the peoples of the world community.

(xix)   Try to popularize the aims of Acharya Tulsi's Anuvrat Movement and observe Anuvrat Code of Conduct.

6. Political Action

(i)   Support the emergence of a world government with due involvement of all regions of the world and resources of peace and material at command.

(ii)   Reach people with power and encourage them to act nonviolently.

(iii)   Demand exchange of children (including children of leaders) for short visits when the tension between two or more countries escalates (Peace Children).

(ix)   Make injustices visible to all sections of society.

(v)   Support political candidates footed on a peace platform.

(vi)   Create conditions for conscientious objection or status as an alternative to military service.

(vii)   Organize, train and utilize a world peace brigade to be deployed in potential areas of conflict.

(viii) See that its members enter political process as nonviolence candidates with peace platforms.

(ix)   Address and meekly redress/remove political/economic or social causes of poverty, which contribute to violence.

(x)   Stress urgent need for religious institutions to enter into dialogue so that they no longer remain causes of violence.

(xi)   Support global action on local successful movements of peace (like Chipko or Anuvrat Movement) to protect the global environment and promote peace through individual commitment.

7. Legal Action

(i)   Explore legal defences available for participating in civil disobedience struggle(s) using the possibility of World citizenship as a method.

(ii)   Advocate and uphold the right to choose political allegiance taking advantage of arguments in accordance with the Universal Declaration of Human Rights.

The above action plan for the eradication of violence and promotion of peace and nonviolence was adopted unanimously by the delegates at the concluding session of the International Conference on Peace and Nonviolent Action. It was modified and amended before its acceptance by delegates. It came to be known as the Ladnum Declaration. Originally the draft was prepared by a committee chosen by the delegates comprising the following members:
Mr Garry Davis (USA)
President, World Government of World Citizens Washington, USA

Mr S. L. Gandhi (India)
Secretary, ANUVIBHA and Coordinator of the Conference, Jaipur
Dr (Mrs) Suman Khanna (India)
Assistant Professor, Matasunmderi College, Delhi
Dr Ramjee Singh (India)
Head, Dept of Gandhian Thought, Bhagalpur University, Bhagalpur (Bihar)
Rev Monika Sidenmark (Sweden)
Cooperation for Peace, Vallingby Sweden
Shirley O'Key (USA)
Grandmothers for Peace, Sacramento, USA
Ataur Rahman (Bangladesh)
Society for Peace and Development, Rajoir Bangladesh
It was finalized with the help of Mr J. N. Puri and Mr Vinod Seth by
S. L. Gandhi, Convener of the Conference.

2. Rajsamand Declaration

The second International Conference was held at Rajsamand, India from 17 to 21 February 1991. Attached to the general statement, there is a useful outline of a Suggested Course for Training in Nonviolence.

Declaration on Nonviolence

Peace is not merely the absence of war nor nonviolence only abstinence from physical violence. It is a holistic and positive concept encompassing all manifestations of life and society on the Earth. It includes both structural peace and ecological balance. Nonviolence implies active and dynamic love, respect and reverence for all living beings that inhabit this planet, attributes of equality, human dignity, poise, harmony and resistance to tyranny and injustice.

Need of Training in Nonviolence

For the past many years, humankind has evolved and invented numerous methods of training in violence and war. We have been spending enormous material and human resources on them at the cost of mass hunger, illiteracy and environmental damage. Besides, violence has been growing menacingly in different forms. The complexity of the situation that the world faces today makes it mandatory for us to move further from the principle of peaceful coexistence towards a more active principle of cooperation for peace and develop the requisite instruments for such cooperation. Hence, training in nonviolence is imperative in modern times. If we fail to evolve a viable scientific system to train and orient people in ahimsa, we shall be failing in our most important duty towards humanity and society.

Content of the Training in Nonviolence

To train people in nonviolence, we must combine the aspects of both individual and community growth and build an integrated personality with appropriate training of hand, head and heart which will facilitate the structural and functional excellence of social development. The objective of this training is to enable all peoples to gain an insightful understanding of nonviolence and peace and the spiritual values on which they rest, equip them with skills for individual and mass nonviolent action, prepare them for democratic leadership in conflict resolution through nonviolence and help them develop positive attitudes for harmonious living.

Strategies, Tools and Organization of Training in Nonviolence

We seek participation of concerned young people from all over the world. Training in nonviolence has both its individual and social dimensions. It should employ such methods as meditation to bring about a change of heart and attitude in the individuals, persuasion, personal example, willingness to suffer rather than injure another, moral uprightness, practice of sharing one's resources with the other, faith in the essential goodness of all humans and regard for the basic human rights of all. The other tools of training may include regular classes, lectures, self-study, workshops, panel discussions, community living, games and sanitation. Training should encourage constructive programmes and social service. It should also take special care of developing the ability among the trainees to understand the pulse of the people, public opinion, training in communications and in audio-visual programmes. Equally essential is the training in the organization and leadership of nonviolent action. It involves investigation of the problem, negotiation, conciliation, arbitration and other processes of conflict resolution such as mobilization of opinion, planning, preparation, use of different forms of nonviolent direct action including non-cooperation, civil disobedience and fasting, etc.

The Global Role of Education in Peace and Nonviolence

Education is the most important instrument of training in nonviolence because it shapes and moulds the human mind. Training in nonviolence and peace should be introduced in education both at the formal and informal levels to bring about an attitudinal transformation.

Recommendations

We make the following recommendations and declare that their adoption by the institutions and individuals of the world will pave the way for a peaceful and nonviolent world order:

1. UNESCO, National Governments and Voluntary Organizations working in the field of education as well as in the other areas of human welfare should evolve a programme to introduce global peace education and training in nonviolence both at the formal and informal levels of education.
2. We the delegates to the second ICPNA who have helped in the formulation of this Declaration take upon us and recommend that all non-governmental organizations should endeavour to create awareness of the importance of nonviolence at all social levels in order that there might be a strong public opinion against expenditure on armaments and war, leading to a political determination gradually to abolish the institutions of war and in their place establish institutions of peace.

Training and Orientation in the Conceptual Understanding of Ahimsa

(i)   *Change of Heart: The Training of the Mind*

Human emotions like greed, fear, enmity, antagonism, vanity, cruelty, intolerance, absolutism in thought and action, desire for excessive consumption, abuse of environment, aggression between peoples, absence of a feeling of holism of the universe and the planet are responsible for violence and war. In order to bring about a change of heart, the individual must first gain in insightful understanding of the factors that lead to the rise of these tendencies in him and the means with which they can be curbed, controlled, refined and sublimated. The human mind needs to be thoroughly researched as the seeds of both *ahimsa* (nonviolence) and *himsa* (violence) take their roots in it. The training of the mind precedes all other things in a course meant for the training of people in ahimsa.

(ii)   *Inculcation of Cosmic Values: A Holistic Perspective*

This course is proposed to be geared to the needs of a nonviolent sociopolitical world order. The members of the global community ought to be trained and oriented in such a way that human and cosmic values like detachment towards the body and matter, fearlessness, friendship, forgiveness, humility, compassion, communal harmony, tolerance of divergent views, relative thinking, relative behaviour, positive attitudes, selflessness, a sense of universal responsibility towards the world as an integral whole, abstinence from harming nature, respect for inherent human rights, consumption of resources in keeping with the satisfaction of the basic needs of all on which depend peace and sustainable development may blossom in them naturally. The above values can not be imposed on an individual from outside. They exist in all human beings but are often dormant. They must be awakened.

(iii)   *The State of Good Health: A Prerequisite for the Growth of Nonviolence*

The following symptoms indicate lack of good health and it has been noticed that they give rise to violence. They include low percentage of glucose in the blood, the malfunctioning of spleen and liver, hyperacidity, inbalanced diet, etc. The removal of these factors will result in the growth of ahimsa.

(iv) *Healthy Economy: A Must for the Ushering in of a Nonviolent Society*
The inculcation of such values as renunciation, non-acquisitiveness, decentralized economy, honesty in earning a living, desire for sharing in resources and consumption according to one's need will promote healthy economy and pave the way for the creation of a nonviolent society.

(v) *Transformation of Human Relationships*
One should refrain from behaving cruelly with the other. The relationship between the employers and the members of a family should be cordial and harmonious. Training in co-existence, mutual adjustment and positive outlook will be imparted.

(vi) *Components of the Training in Ahimsa*
Faith in the purity of means and all the aspects of Preksha Dhyan (perceptive meditation) like Pranayam (breathing exercises), Kayotsarg (relaxation with self-awareness) perception of breathing, Leshya Dhyan (colour meditation), perception of psychic centres, Anupreksha (therapeutic thinking), a unique technique to develop the innate traits of human nature like fearlessness, tolerance, self-reliance, friendship, detachment, humility, compassion and communal harmony are some of the components of the training in ahimsa.

(B) Practical Training Based on Innovative Experiments

It will include practice, exercises and experiments in control of human emotions, promotion of the dignity of labour, fearlessness, tolerance, self-restraint, tapasya (austerity) and detachment.

10

Global Survival

The Global Forum on Human Survival brings together spiritual and parliamentary leaders, together with scientists, artists and leading members of other disciplines, in an effort to save the planet. The origin of the Global Forum was a meeting at Tarrytown House near New York, sponsored by the Temple of Understanding and the Global Committee of Parlimentarians. Two international forums have so far been held: one in Oxford in 1988 and the second in Moscow in 1990. Distinguished leaders, drawn from all religions, have taken part in an individual capacity.

1. Oxford Declaration

For Global Survival

The Final Statement of the Oxford Conference

We have met at Oxford bringing together our individual experience from the parliaments and religious traditions of the world – and from the media, the sciences, business, education and the arts. We were brought together by a common concern for global survival, and have entered into a new dialogue on our common future.

This meeting is a timely convergence of hearts, minds and events. Human society is in a period of intense introspection, gripped by fear, uncertainty and confusion. But we are challenged by new opportunities and encouraged by signs of hope.

We recognize that it is not only human survival but the survival of the whole planet, with all its interdependent forms of life, which is threatened. The earth, as recent environmental evidence confirms, is delicately balanced and vulnerable. Each one of us must accept the responsibility to care for and protect the earth, which is our home.

We have derived from our meeting a vivid awareness of the essential oneness of humanity, and also the realization that each human person has both a spiritual and a political dimension. We acknowledge the inadequacy of attitudes and institutions within all our traditions to deal with our present global crisis.

We therefore now affirm our shared vision of survival, and we commit ourselves to work for a fundamentally changed and better world. We urge the leaders of the world to adopt new attitudes and to implement new policies based on sustainability and justice.

We have explored the nature of the relationship between political and religious life, and as parliamentarians and spiritual leaders we have agreed that we both need and desire to work together. We have spoken frankly of the care that must be taken to listen to, and not exploit one another. We invite our brothers and sisters from the fields of education, journalism, the arts and other channels of communication to become our partners as we begin to develop together concrete plans of action at all levels.

We have worked together to formulate specific proposals. These include:

1. At the global level we commit ourselves to choose and to promote styles of life which will sustain our earth, sky and sea for future generations; if we are to have a common future, we must act as responsible world citizens as well as loyal citizens of a particular nation.

2. Where international or civic relationships are broken by conflict or injustice, we commit ourselves to promoting reconciliation and peace; if we are to achieve common security, we must dismantle arms, build trust and join in the struggle to enhance the quality of human life.

3. Where opportunities for practical cooperation exist within nations or local communities, we shall avoid jealous competition and promote respectful and equal partnerships of young and old, women and men, of people of all races, religions, traditional cultures and political persuasions.

4. Where misunderstandings or ignorance keep us apart we shall develop in both public and private sectors modes of education, communication and dialogue, which can provide ethical and moral motivation and appropriate technical methods.

5. While we strive for basic human rights, which should be inspired by our religious teachings and safeguarded by our political systems, we shall also exercise our human duties as individuals and communities to protect our earth and to protect each other.

6. Three areas of present critical concern shall receive our special attention: 1. Elimination of the perils of nuclear and other armaments; 2. the realization of appropriate balances between resources and populations; and 3. promotion of the well-being of vulnerable groups, particularly women and children.

In order to implement these proposals we shall support existing structures, such as the United Nations agencies, and shall promote at regional, national and local levels all possible collaboration between spiritual leaders and parliamentarians. As participants in this Oxford Global Survival Conference, we commit ourselves to revive neglected ideals, revitalize useful structures and, where necessary, devise, at every level, new ways to coordinate our work and improve our communication.

Each one of us has been changed by our Oxford experience. We have clarified our objectives and undertake commitments that are irrevocable. We know that we will be continually tested. We pledge to share the positive results of this conference with all people. Let us do so together with determination, love and compassion.

2. Moscow Declaration

The environment that sustains life on Earth is in peril. Human actions are responsible.

We, the participants at the Global Forum of Spiritual and Parliamentary Leaders assembled in Moscow in January 1990, coming from diverse nations, cultures, religions and traditions, are conscious of sharing a common humanity. In the spirit of love and mutual respect that prevailed at our previous meeting at Oxford, we have reached agreement on the threats to our common future. We commit ourselves to action and have identified some clear directions for such action. We urge the governments and peoples of the Earth to confront these unprecedented dangers squarely and courageously.

The future of humanity and of our fellow creatures is at stake. We human beings have become a danger to ourselves. We must act in time. And, we must now adopt a new planetary perspective. We need to understand our immense and recently acquired power to alter nature. Technological solutions are indispensable, but they alone are not enough. We must accept responsibility for adopting a spritually wise, technologically sound, ethical and farsighted stewardship of the planet – and a renewed respect for Nature on which all life depends.

This is an issue that transcends national, ideological and generational divisions. It has the potential to unify our species in dealing with our common peril. Our loyalties must go beyond narrow frontiers to all life on Earth.

This crisis we face is also an opportunity filled with promise. There is a groundswell of hope for the future inspired by the demolition of the Berlin Wall, the successes of people in many lands in ridding themselves of oppressive regimes, the beginnings of disarmament and the end of the Cold War. Let us harness this newly released human energy and hope, moving beyond our preoccupation with military security to embrace the larger reality of ecological security for the sake of global survival.

The world of tomorrow belongs to the children of today. High school students participated in the Forum to remind us that young and old must share the global class-room.

Our action must be founded on clear principles and understanding:

Time is short, and the problems are profound; courage, imagination and sustained commitment are essential. Business as usual will not do: radical change in our ideas and our attitudes is overdue.

There is now a wide consensus on the seriousness and urgency of the problems we face. The time has come for action.

The problems must be tackled by the joint efforts of individuals throughout the world. Also, the spiritual community, parliaments, governments, international and non-governmental organizations, the business community, intellectuals, artists, communicators, and educators must all accept their responsibilities in a concerted effort.

We must find a new spiritual and ethical basis for human activities on Earth: humankind must enter into a new communion with Nature, and regain respect for the wonders of the natural world.

World peace, the full and equal participation of women and men, fairness, the elimination of poverty and a determination to protect our children from preventable disease and death, are essential conditions for sustainable, environmentally sound development in our interdependent world.

Concern with the environment must become pervasive at every level of decision-making, from the personal to the global. Indeed, there are critical links between the pressure of a growing world population with legitimate aspirations for a decent life, freedom from the pollution of abiding poverty, intolerable debt, and a deteriorating environment. The number of human beings has been growing at an unprecedented rate. The limited carrying capacity of the earth's ecosystem cannot sustain a limitless number of human beings at any given time. Therefore, a population policy is an essential component of any effective, long-range environmental strategy.

An integrated strategy for sustainable development, which strives to improve the quality of life and eradicate poverty, must include the education of women and girls and raise their role and status to full equality. The extent to which women are free to make responsible decisions affecting their lives and those of their families is crucial to achieving a sustainable balance between population growth, accessible resources and the life environment.

We must together learn how to live in greater harmony with our planet than we have so far done. This is the primordial challenge which now confronts all of us.

The human race has never had greater economic, scientific and technological potential. We must find the will and the means to use it – for life.

There needs to be greater understanding and dialogue, particularly between scientists and spiritual leaders. We also recognize the key role of political decision-makers, media communicators, artists, the business community, and organized labour.

We must work towards the elimination of all weapons of mass destruction.

We must have the courage to question established ideas, doctrines, techniques and assumptions. We must have the imagination and the will to make new environmentally sound ideas and technologies fully accessible to all, especially at the grass roots.

We call for a comprehensive international treaty to protect the natural environment.

We must innovate in the field of international and national institutions so that we can act coherently and effectively, such as: establishing an Environmental Security Council, and designing new economic and social indicators so as to give proper consideration to the quality of life as well as the value of the natural environment.

We consider it imperative that the cultures and habitats of indigenous peoples be respected and protected. All can learn from their ways of life.

We must have the vision and the resolution to make financial resources available on a scale commensurate with the critical importance of the problems we face.

We pledge ourselves to work for these high purposes in the interests of humanity and of our fragile planet. As a symbol of our pledge, each of us promises to plant a tree this very year, and tell people why.

An Earth Charter

In June 1992, in Rio de Janeiro, Brazil, a United Nations Conference on Environment and Development (UNCED) will proclaim an Earth Charter which is intended to set the principles on which human society in the future must be based. It is imperative that all peoples participate in and contribute to the creation of this document, for a charter must be something that we all basically believe in if it is to direct our values and actions. This document is a contribution to the Earth Charter from the religious community of North America, composed by fifty representatives from all the major faiths. It will be part of an ongoing discussion within the religious world in the process toward UNCED. It could also be an instrument for creating a groundswell that will culminate in the united voice of the world's peoples that will demand from the UN Conference the decisions that are essential for our common future.

An Earth Charter
A Religious Perspective

International Coordinating Committee on Religion and the Earth

This document is the distillation of a series of consultations held throughout the world, organized by the International Coordinating Committee on Religion and the Earth (ICCRE) to elicit contributions from the religions of the world, toward the creation of an Earth Charter. Meetings took place in North America, Europe, Asia, the Philippines and Africa. This final document will be offered to the United Nations Conference on Environment and Development (UNCED, June 1992) for the purpose of influencing the Earth Charter that this 'Earth Summit' will adopt. It will also stand in its own right as an interfaith perspective on the crisis we face and the future we must create.

Spiritual Principles

Interdependence

The Earth is an interdependent community of life. All parts of this system are interconnected and essential to the functioning of the whole.

The Value of Life

Life is sacred. Each of the diverse forms of life has its own intrinsic value.

Beauty

Earth and all forms of life embody beauty. The beauty of the Earth is food for the human spirit. It inspires human consciousness with wonder, joy and creativity.

Humility

Human beings are not outside or above the community of life. We have not woven the web of life; we are but a strand within it. We depend on the whole for our very existence.

Responsibilities

Human beings have a special capacity to affect the ecological balance. In awareness of the consequences of each action, we have a special responsibility to preserve life in its integrity and diversity and to avoid destruction and waste for trivial or merely utilitarian reasons.

Rights

Every human being has the right to a healthy environment. We must grant this right to others: both those living today and the generations to come.

Ethics for Living

Sustainably

Human beings must live in a way that meets the needs of the present without compromising the ability of future generations to meet their own needs.

Justly

Sufficiently
In a world of great disparities between rich and poor, justice demands that every human being be able to obtain the basic needs of life.

In Participation
Justice demands universal participation in all aspects of a sustainable society through legal and institutional structures.
In Solidarity
Sustainability with justice will only be achieved through an ethic of global solidarity, which includes the rights of future generations.

Peacefully

The sacredness of life demands the practice of non-violence; differences must be resolved by consultation rather than conflict. War and the production of weapons destroys the environment as well as human life.

Simply

To establish economic justice, people in the industrialized world must learn to live more frugally. Simplicity of life fosters both inner freedom and outer sustainability.

Knowledgeably

Environmental education and free access to information are essential for global awareness and skilful care of the Earth.

Holistically

Human life, to be fully human, must include physical, intellectual, moral and spiritual development within the community of all life.

Programme Areas

Our concern for all life expresses itself not only in our prayers and in statements of principles, but in actions in our personal, professional and political lives. We, representatives of the world's religious communities, recommend action in the following programme areas. We also call upon our members to develop actions around these areas, and to promote and implement them in their personal and professional lives.

Local and Individual Level

1. Education
The promotion of environmental education as an integral and compulsory part of school curricula.
2. Health
The promotion of environmental education as a mandatory component of all health care, both in medical schools and in medical practice.

3. Food production
The promotion of sustainable farming systems as the basis of all agricultural food production, including the preservation and integration of indigenous methods and indigenous foods.

4. Food consumption
The promotion of food consumption that is lower on the food chain (less energy consuming), as well as food that is organically, humanely and locally produced.

5. Energy
The promotion of sustainable patterns of energy consumption through net reduction, increased efficiency and minimal use of fossil fuels.

6. Transport
The promotion of transport forms that are less energy consuming and less polluting.

7. Wildlife
The protection and, where necessary, the restoration of biological diversity, and the revival of the traditional peaceful co-existence between people and wild animals.

8. Family and Community
The promotion of the 'extended family' or similar forms of community as the basic unit for integrated and environmentally balanced living.

9. Population
The promotion of population education toward the reduction of birth rates, and the related appreciation of economic and social factors.

10. Grassroots Movements
The promotion of grassroots movements to protect the environment from vested interests of all kinds (i.e. the Chipko Movement in India).

11. Religious Traditions
The promotion of religious traditions and practices that foster concern and responsibility for the environment, and the challenging of those that do not. This would include the protection and restoration of many of the indigenous values and practices which have a particular contribution to make in this area.

12. Regional Policies
The promotion of regional policies and legislation that would consider not only local effects, but also the impact on the rest of the world.

13. Local Government
The development of local government policies and structures for the promotion of the above programmes.

International Level

1. International Wealth
The redistribution of land, wealth and natural resources for the good of many. This will require a restructuring of the present economic system that would

include the promotion of 'quality of life indicator', rather than simply measures of quantity, and address the issue of debt and world trade agreements.

2. A Transnational Approach

The establishment of procedures and mechanisms that would permit a transnational approach to environmental issues and disputes, including standards, accountability and enforcement.

3. Transnational Sharing

The promotion of appropriate technology exchange: new technology from the industrialized countries and indigenous technology from the poorer nations.

4. Finances

The creation of a 'world fund' for the protection of the environment: money to be raised through projects like, 'energy taxation', an 'Earth stamp', etc.

5. Transnational Corporations

The limitation of the power of transnational corporations, as well as the encouragement of their enormous ability to foster justice and sustainability.

6. Militarization

The promotion of complete disarmament, the termination of all weapon production and trade, and the ending of military technology transfer.

7. Science

The encouragement of scientists to be environmentally responsible and to use their knowledge and skill to help alleviate environmental problems.

8. Media

The promotion of mass/electronic media for the development of ecological attitudes, values and skills.

9. Women and Children

The promotion of full and equal participation of women in all government and non-governmental organizations, in decision-making, implementation, administration and funding at international, national and community levels. The protection of women and children as the most vulnerable to environmental and economic injustice.

10. Indigenous Peoples

The support of indigenous peoples in their efforts to protect their natural environments, and the recognition of the special contribution of indigenous peoples in providing vital wisdom and leadership in resisting the forces that are destroying the earth.

11. Biotechnology

Contribution to the ethical process involved in the development and application of biotechnology and genetic engineering.

12. Wilderness

The promotion of protection of remaining habitat (forests, wetlands, rivers, estuaries, etc.) through wilderness preservation and sustainable life practices.

The World's Religions for the World's Children

*Prior to the World Summit for Children held at the United Nations in September
1990, a Conference on The World's Religions for the World's Children was held
at Princeton, USA by the World Conference on Religion and Peace. It was
attended by 150 people from 40 countries drawn from all major religions.*

Declaration of World Religious Leaders

The World's Religions for the World's Children

Princeton, New Jersey, 25–27 July 1990

Conscious of the plight of vast numbers of children throughout the world, we
representatives of twelve religions from forty countries participating in the
World's Religions for the World's Children conference, meeting in
Princeton, New Jersey, USA, 25–27 July 1990, speak with common voice. We
commend the United Nations for its efforts in creating and adopting the
Convention on the Rights of the Child. We urge its ratification and adherence
in practice by all governments. We commend those government leaders who
have recognized the urgency and priority of addressing the needs and rights of
children. Cognizant of the efforts of earlier generations represented by the
1924 League of Nations Geneva Declaration on the Rights of the Child, and
the United Nations 1959 Declaration on the Rights of the Child, we are aware
of the difficulty of moving from the statement of rights to their realization. Our
common voice resounds despite differences in our traditions, our practices,
our beliefs, and despite our inadequacies. Our religious traditions summon us
to regard the child as more than a legal entity. The sacredness of life compels
us to be a voice of conscience. We speak hereby to heads of state and
government, to the United Nations, to our religious communities and to all,
throughout the world, who have held a child in love, with joy for its life, with
tears for its pain.

Recognizing the Rights of the Child

The Convention on the Rights of the Child, which acknowledges the rights of the world's children to survival, protection and development, is rooted in the Universal Declaration of Human Rights which recognizes the inherent dignity and the equal and inalienable rights of all members of the human family. We recognize that, lamentably, such rights are not universally respected or legally guaranteed, nor are they always accepted as moral obligations.

As religious men and women, however, we dare to assert that the state of childhood, with its attendant vulnerability, dependence, and potential, founds a principle that the human community must give children's basic needs priority over competing claims – and a 'first-call' – upon the human and material resources of our societies. Such a principle needs to be both recognized and accepted as a guide for relevant actions in human communities.

Society's Responsibility to Children

The survival, protection, and development of children is the responsibility of the whole world community. However, for countless girls and boys there is no survival, no protection, no chance for development. Societies are morally bound to address the obscene conditions which result in the death of fourteen million children during every year, two thirds from preventable causes, and the other conditions of abject poverty that result in wasted bodies, stunted physical development, or permanent handicaps. Existing health care knowledge and technology, promptly and persistently applied, have the potential to make dramatic improvements in child survival and health with relatively moderate financial costs. Such possibilities underscore our obligations. To fail to make such efforts for the well-being of children is morally unconscionable.

Societies are also bound to rectify the gross injustices and violations which children suffer, such as child abuse, sexual and labour exploitation, homelessness, victimization due to war and the tragic consequences of family disintegration, cultural genocide, social deprivations stemming from intolerance based upon race, sex, age, or religion, to name but a few. Addressing these issues will require fundamental structural change.

Societies are obliged to confront the broad constellation of human forces and failures which affect children. The social and international order necessary for the full realization of children's rights does not exist. Our interdependent political and economic systems can be restructured and refined to provide children their basic need. The world has the resources to provide the basic needs of children. Wars, in which children are increasingly the victims and even the targets of violence, need not be the inevitable expression of human conflict. Our readiness to resolve conflict through violent means can be changed. Development cannot succeed under the illusion that our resources are inexhaustible or uniformly self-renewing.

While our air, water, and soil are polluted, we still have the chance to reverse the most devastating trends of environmental degradation. What will we bequeath to our children? The dangerous forces that impact upon children jeopardize the full realization of freedom, justice and peace.

The grim realities we confront demand our outrage because they exist; they demand our repentance because they have been silently tolerated or even justified; they demand our response because all can be addressed, some of them quite readily.

The Responsibilities of Governments and International Organizations

We religious women and men gathered in Princeton urge governments and relevant international organizations to fulfil their responsibilities to children through at least the following:

To sign, ratify, fully implement, and monitor compliance with the Convention on the Rights of the Child.

To undertake those actions which would have a dramatic impact upon child survival at very low cost.

To take vigorous and immediate action to rectify the myriad obscene injustices which children suffer, such as abuse from exploitation.

To take the steps necessary, in each country, to achieve the goals for children and development in the 1990s, as defined by the international community.

To utilize peaceful means of conflict resolution in order to protect children from the ravages of war.

To create new, or adjust existing, political and economic structures that can provide access to and distribution – for all – of both the natural resources and the products of human labour, including information, so that the claims of justice may be met.

To undertake the bold steps known to be necessary and to develop new steps to protect and reclaim the environment as the heritage for our children and succeeding generations' development.

To allocate adequate funds to undergird the global programmes, addressing health, education and development.

To ensure full participation of Non Governmental Organizations (NGOs) in the implementation of appropriate actions.

To provide basic education for all children.

To reduce the burden of debt that robs a nation's children of their rightful heritage.

To support the family, help keep it intact, and provide the resources and services for the adequate care and protection of its children.

To provide resources and develop programmes for the survival, health, and education of women, the bearers and primary care givers of children.

To ensure the participation of women in the entire range of social governance and decision making.

To take steps to ensure that children actually receive a first call on society's resources.

Religious and Spiritual Responsibilities

Our consciences as religious men and women, including those of us bearing governmental and other forms of social responsibility, will not allow us to evade the responsibilities of our religious traditions. We therefore call upon religious women and men and institutions:

To order our own priorities so as to reaffirm our central claims about the sacredness of life.

To examine any of our own traditional practices that may violate the deeper spirit of our faiths and indeed the sacredness of human life.

To provide resources for families, from single parent to extended in size, so that they can fulfil their roles in spiritual formation and education.

To protect and support parents in their rights and responsibilities as the primary religious educators.

To undertake actions to promote the well-being, education, and leadership roles of female children and their right to equal treatment with male children.

To engage in services of nurture, mercy, education, and advocacy, and to exemplify before the world the possibilities for compassion and care.

To co-operate with all agencies of society, including other religious bodies, that have as their purpose the well-being of the children in our societies.

To advocate the ratification and implementation of the Convention on the Rights of the Child in our respective countries and communities.

To work for the protection of the unborn in accord with the teachings of our respective religious traditions.

To establish independent systems to monitor the state of children's rights.

To co-ordinate with other religions in the removal of religious and other forms of prejudice and conflict in all contexts.

To re-order our communities' resources in accord with the principle of the right of children to a first call on those resources.

Political will is necessary to create the social and international climate in which survival, protection and development can be achieved. We call on governments and the international community to manifest that will. Spiritual will is necessary to establish a shared ethos in which children can flourish in freedom, justice and peace. We call on all spiritual and religious peoples and institutions to manifest that will.

13

The Universal Declaration on Non-Violence

The Universal Declaration on Non-Violence derives from a group of con-templatives of different faiths who, as members of the Snowmass Conference, have met on a regular basis for ongoing contemplative dialogue. Because it was drafted by contemplatives, it is not a 'peace' document in the usual sense. It reflects the insight of the monks that reality is one and that at last this truth is being recognized in the historical process itself. Our new global civilization needs to be based on the spiritual values of love and compassion. By recognizing the right and duty of governments to defend the security of their people and to relieve those afflicted by exploitation and persecution, the document avoids being 'pacifist', but it makes very clear that religions should no longer be accomplices to war, terrorism or any form of violence. Rather, religions should use their influence to help human beings unlearn their tendency to be aggressive and help to make non-violence a pre-eminent value in all human relations.

A Universal Declaration on Non-Violence
The Incompatibility of Religion and War

This document is an attempt to set forth a vision of non-violence within the context of an emerging global civilization in which all forms of violence, especially war, are totally unacceptable as means to settle disputes between and among nations, groups and persons. This new vision of civilization is global in scope, universal in culture, and based on love and compassion, the highest moral spiritual principles of the various historical religions. Its universal nature acknowledges the essential fact of modern life: the interde-pendence of nations, economies, cultures and religious traditions.

As members of religious groups throughout the world, we are increasingly aware of our responsibility to promote peace in our age and in the ages to come. Nevertheless, we recognize that in the history of the human family, people of various religions, acting officially in the name of their respective traditions, have either initiated or collaborated in organized and systematic violence or war. These actions have at times been directed against other religious traditions, groups and nations, as well as within particular religious traditions. This pattern of behaviour is totally inappropriate for spiritual persons and communities. Therefore, as members of world religions, we declare before the human family, that:

Religion can no longer be an accomplice to war, to terrorism, or to any other forms of violence, organized or spontaneous, against any member of the human family. Because this family is one, global and interrelated, our actions must be consistent with this identity. We recognize the right and duty of governments to defend the security of their people and to relieve those afflicted by exploitation and persecution. Nevertheless, we declare that religion must not permit itself to be used by any state, group or organization for the purpose of supporting aggression for nationalistic gain. We have an obligation to promote a new vision of society, one in which war has no place in resolving disputes between and among states, organizations and religions.

In making this declaration, we the signatories commit ourselves to this new vision. We call upon all the members of our respective traditions to embrace this vision. We urge our members and all peoples to use every moral means to disruade their governments from promoting war or terrorism. We strongly encourage the United Nations Organization to employ all available resources toward the development of peaceful methods of resolving conflicts among nations.

Our declaration is meant to promote such a new global society, one in which non-violence is pre-eminent as a value in all human relations. We offer this vision of peace, mindful of the words of Pope Paul VI to the United Nations in November 1965: 'No more war; war never again!'

Notes

Introduction

1. Prince Philip, Preface, p. xiii, in Hans Küng, *Global Responsibility. In Search of a New World Ethic*, SCM Press and Crossroad Publishing Co 1991.
2. Ibid., p. 138.
3. Ibid., p. xiii.
4. Hans Küng, in *World Faiths Insight*, February 1989, p. 15.

The Interfaith Movement: The Present Reality

1. Charles Bonney, quoted in my *Pilgrimage of Hope*, SCM Press and Crossroad Publishing Co 1992, p. 26. The material in this section is drawn from this book.
2. Quoted in *Pilgrimage of Hope*, p. 66.
3. Ibid., pp. 70-1 and 73.
4. Ibid., p. 93.
5. The Kyoto Declaration. Statement of the First Assembly of the World Conference on Religion and Peace held at Kyoto, Japan in October 1970. See below, p. 49.

Are Human Rights Based on Religious Traditions?

1. Quoted by Robert Traer, *Faith in Human Rights*, Georgetown University Press, Washington DC 1991, p. l.
2. See Leonard Swidler, 'Human Rights: A Historical Overview', in *The Ethics of World Religions and Human Rights*, ed. Hans Küng and Jürgen Moltmann, *Concilium* 1990/2, pp. 12ff.
3. Quoted by Leonard Swidler in *Religious Liberty and Human Rights*, ed. Leonard Swidler, Ecumenical Press, Temple University 1986.
4. *Concilium* 1990/2, p. 19. See also my *Children of One God*, Vallentine Mitchell 1991, p. 28.
5. *Pilgrimage of Hope*, pp. 71-2, and *Children of One God*, p. 29.
6. Swidler (ed.), *Religious Liberty and Human Rights*, p. ix.
7. *Concilium* 1990/2, p. 13.
8. *Concilium* 1990/2, p. 26.
9. Traer, *Faith in Human Rights*, p. 101.
10. C. G. Montefiore, *The Origin of Religion as Illustrated by the Ancient Hebrews*, Williams and Norgate 1892, p. 156.
11. Traer, *Faith in Human Rights*, p. 99.
12. Ibid., quoting Rabbi Daniel Polish.
13. Ibid., quoting J.Robert Nelson, p. 20.
14. *Concilium* 1990/2, p. 51.
15. *Concilium* 1990/2, p. 73.

16. T.M.P. Mahadevan, *Outlies of Hinduism*, Chetana, Bombay ²1960, p. 69.
17. Ibid., p. 68.
18. Swidler (ed.), *Religious Liberty and Human Rights*, p. 197.
19. Traer, *Faith in Human Rights*, p. 136.

Religious Support for Human Rights

1. Robert Traer, *Faith in Human Rights*, Georgetown University Press, Washington, D C 1991.
2. Ibid., p. 3.
3. Ibid., p. 3.
4. Ibid., p. 34.
5. Ibid., p. 37.
6. Ibid., p. 78.
7. Ibid., p. 113.
8. Quoted in my *Together to the Truth*, CLS, Madras 1971, p. 139.
9. Traer, *Faith in Human Rights*, p. 207.
10. John Milbank, 'The End of Dialogue', in *Christian Uniqueness Reconsidered*, ed. Gavin D'Costa, Orbis Books 1990.
11. Paul Knitter in *The Myth of Christian Uniqueness*, ed. John Hick and Paul Knitter, Orbis Books and SCM Press 1988.
12. Hans Küng, *Global Responsibility*, SCM Press and Crossroad Publishing Company 1991, p. 90.

What do the Statements Say?

1. Hans Küng, *Global Responsibility*, SCM Press and Crossroad Publishing Company 1991, p. 37.

The Universal Declaration of Human Rights

1. See, for example, the influence of Monsignor Roncalli, subsequently Pope John XXIII, *Concilium*1990/2, p. 21. See Robert Traer, *Faith in Human Rights*, p. 67.

Declaration on the Elimination of All Forms of Intolerance

1. See The Report on the Declaration of Dr. Homer A. Jack to the World Conference on Religion and Peace, and *World Faiths Insight* 4,1981/2, p. 21.
2. The bracketed inclusive language is added or substituted by the editor, Leonard Swidler.

Fundamental Postulates of Christianity and Judaism

1. See further my *Children of One God*, Vallentine Mitchell 1991, pp.118–19.

The World Conference on Religion and Peace

1. Thanks largely to the initiative of Dr Homer Jack, Secretary General of WCRP,

the UN eventually adopted 'The Declaration on the Elimination of All Forms of Intolerance and of Discrimination Based on Religions or Belief', *Religion and Peace*, WCRP, July 1977 and June 1981.

An Earth Charter

1. The Earth Charter is co-ordinated by International Coordinating Committee on Religion and the Earth, PO Box 67, Greenwich, Connecticut 06830 – 0767, USA.

Addresses

The addresses of the organizations which produced the documents are given below:

1 & 2. The United Nations, UN Plaza, New York 10017, USA

3. The International Council of Christians and Jews, Martin Buber House, Werlestr.2, 6148 Heppenheim, PO Box 129, Germany

4 & 12. World Conference on Religion and Peace, 777 United Nations Plaza, New York, NY 10017, USA

5. The International Association for Religious Freedom, Dreieichstrasse 59, D–6000 Frankfurt 70, Germany

6. Temple of Understanding, Cathedral of St John the Divine, 1047 Amsterdam Ave at 112th St, New York, NY 10025, USA

7. Global Co-operation for a Better World, The Brahma Kumaris Spiritual University, Mt Abu, Rajasthan, India

8. Dr Abelardo Brenes, University of Peace, PO Box 199–1250, Escazu, Costa Rica, Central America

9. Anuvrat Global Organization, Vishwa Shanti Nilayam, PO Box 26, Rajsamand 313 326, India

10. Global Forum of Spiritual and Parliamentary Leaders, 304 East 45th Street, New York, NY 10017, USA

11. An Earth Charter is co-ordinated by the International Co-ordinating Committee on Religion and the Earth, PO Box 67, Greenwich, Connecticut, 06830–0767, USA

13. A Universal Declaration on Non-Violence is co-ordinated by Monastic Interreligious Dialogue, North American Board for East–West Dialogue, Saint Benedict's Convent, Saint Joseph, 56374–0277, USA